Introduction

Whether you are a beginner at sewing or an advanced stitcher with years of experience, you are sure to love the quick and easy projects in *Weekend Sewing*. There are projects for any room and every occasion, making it a perfect go-to for last-minute gifts or a quick weekend project. This book truly has something for everyone. We have included time icons to let you know how long each project may take you to complete, so you can choose projects based on how much time you have available. We hope you enjoy these projects as much as we enjoyed putting them together for you!

Warm regards,

Table of Contents

- 2   Flower Pocket Pincushion
- 5   Sew Cozies
- 11   Sewing Machine Cover
- 14   Sewing Machine Organizer Pad
- 18   Ironing Board Caddy
- 21   Thread Spools Pincushion
- 25   Tricolor Table Topper
- 28   Daisy Fields Table Set
- 34   Summer Fun Mug Rugs
- 40   Bright Blocks Pot Holders
- 44   Microwave Cozies
- 47   Fresh Bread Bag
- 50   Floral Fabric Baskets
- 56   Flower Eyeglasses Case
- 59   Change Purse
- 63   Quilting Basics

Flower Pocket Pincushion

Design by Chris Malone

This sweet pincushion has a padded pocket for all the extras that you may need when you are sewing. Slip a small pair of scissors inside with other supplies like thread and a ruler, and use the edge to hold clips.

Skill Level
Beginner

Finished Size
Pincushion Size: 6" x 6" x 2"

Materials
- Scraps green and gold dot
- Fat eighth each red text, ivory text and blue dot
- 1 each 4½" x 6½" and 5" x 10" batting rectangles
- 1 (⅞") cover button kit
- Cotton or polyester stuffing
- Fusible web with paper release
- Template material
- Thread
- Basic sewing tools and supplies

Project Notes
Read all instructions before beginning this project.

Stitch right sides together using a ¼" seam allowance unless otherwise specified.

Materials and cutting lists assume 20" of usable fabric width for fat eighths.

Cutting

From red text print:
- Cut 2 (6½") B squares.

From ivory text print:
- Cut 2 (4½" x 6½") A rectangles.

Completing the Pincushion

1. Layer the same-size batting and A rectangles, right sides facing, and stitch together on one long side as shown in Figure 1. Trim batting close to the seam and flip the top rectangle over so the batting is in the middle; press the seam flat. Topstitch ¼" from the seam through all layers.

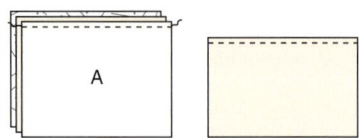

Figure 1

2. Prepare a stem, leaf and petal template using the patterns provided.

3. Referring to Raw-Edge Fusible Appliqué on page 64, draw the stem and leaf on the paper side of the fusible web. Apply the fusible web to the wrong side of the green dot fabric. Cut out the shapes on the pattern lines and remove the paper backing.

4. Referring to Figure 2, arrange the stem and leaf on the front of the pocket about 1¾" from the left edge and the leaf about 1¼" from the bottom. Fuse in place. Machine blanket-stitch around the edges of the appliqués using matching thread.

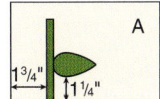

Figure 2

5. Place the pocket on the bottom edge of one B square, matching the raw edges. Baste in place.

6. Place the remaining B square over the pincushion front, right sides facing, and sew all around, leaving a 3" opening at the top. Trim the corners and turn right side out.

7. Stuff the pincushion firmly. Fold in the seam allowances on the opening and slip-stitch the folded edges together to close.

8. Draw the petal pattern six times on the wrong side of the blue dot fabric, leaving about ½" between the shapes. Fold the fabric in half with the pattern on top and pin to remaining batting rectangle as shown in Figure 3. Sew all around on the pattern lines, leaving open at the bottom straight edge. Cut out each petal about ⅛" from the seam, trim the batting close to the seam and clip the curves. Turn right side out and press the edges flat.

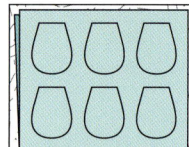

Figure 3

9. Referring to Figure 4 and photo, using white thread, sew a running stitch close to the seam on each petal.

Figure 4

Figure 5

10. Using a doubled length of matching thread, sew a few running stitches across the bottom of a petal. Pull the thread to gather the petal base and pick up a second petal and repeat as shown in Figure 5. Continue adding petals until all six are on the thread and then insert the needle back into the base of the first petal and pull to gather, forming a flower with a small hole in the center. Knot and clip thread.

11. Follow manufacturer's directions to cover the button with the gold dot.

12. Referring to the Placement Diagram and photo, place the flower at the top of the stem. Knot a doubled length of thread and come up from the inside of the pocket, through the flower center and through the shank on the covered button. Go back through the flower center and through the pocket lining to attach the flower. ●

Flower Pocket Pincushion
Placement Diagram 6" x 6" x 2"

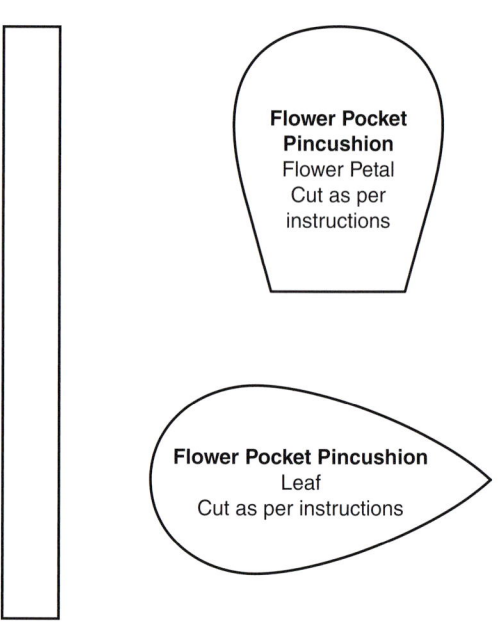

Flower Pocket Pincushion
Flower Petal
Cut as per instructions

Flower Pocket Pincushion
Leaf
Cut as per instructions

Flower Pocket Pincushion
Stem
Cut as per instructions

Sew Cozies

Designs by Chris Malone

Canning jars are great for storing small sewing supplies, and these cute cozies are the perfect way to decorate them.

Skill Level
Beginner

Sew Jacket

Finished Size
Sew Jacket: 12" x 4½"

Materials
- Scraps red, gold and green dot
- Scrap brown felt
- 1 fat quarter ivory text print
- 1 (5" x 12½") batting rectangle
- ¾ yard jumbo red rickrack
- Ivory No. 8 pearl cotton thread or embroidery floss
- 1 (6¾" tall x 12" circumference) widemouthed glass canning jar with lid and ring
- Template material
- Fusible web with paper release
- 2½" length elastic cord
- ⅝" diameter cover button kit
- Fabric glue
- Thread
- Basic sewing tools and supplies

Project Notes
Read all instructions before beginning this project.

Stitch right sides together using a ¼" seam allowance unless otherwise specified.

Materials and cutting lists assume 20" of usable fabric width for fat quarters and eighths.

Cutting
Prepare pieces for fusible appliqué referring to Raw-Edge Fusible Appliqué on page 64.

From ivory text print:
- Cut 2 (5" x 12½") A rectangles and 1 (5") B circle.

Completing the Sew Jacket
1. Prepare templates for the word "sew" using the patterns provided.

2. Trace the letter patterns onto the paper side of the fusible web. Cut shapes apart and apply to the wrong side of the fabrics listed below. Cut out on pattern lines and remove paper backing.

- Red dot: s
- Gold dot: e
- Green dot: w

3. Arrange the letters in the center of one A rectangle and fuse in place. Machine blanket-stitch around each appliqué using matching thread.

4. Cut the rickrack in half and pin one length down the length of the appliquéd strip just below the letters. Attach the rickrack by working a French knot through each peak of the trim as shown in Figure 1. Trim any excess at the ends. Repeat with the second length of rickrack above the letters.

Figure 1

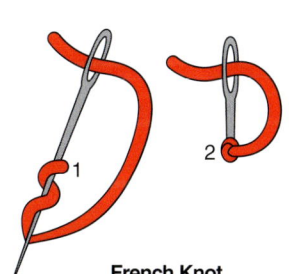

French Knot

AnniesCraftStore.com

5. Referring to Figure 2, fold the elastic cord in half to form a loop and place the ends at the end of the appliquéd jacket front. Stitch across to hold, backstitching a few times to make it secure.

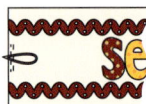

Figure 2

6. Layer batting and remaining A rectangle, right side up, and appliquéd rectangle, right side down, and pin. Sew around all sides, leaving a 3" opening on one long side. Trim the batting close to the seam and trim the corners. Turn right side out, pulling the cord outward, and press the edges flat. Fold in the seam allowance on the opening and slip-stitch the folded edges together to close.

7. Topstitch all around close to the seam.

8. Follow the manufacturer's directions to apply red dot fabric to the cover button.

9. Wrap the jacket around the jar and mark where the button should be sewn on the opposite end of the jacket as shown in Figure 3. Sew button securely in place.

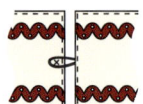

Figure 3

10. Thread needle with a doubled length of thread and sew a gathering stitch all around the fabric circle. Remove the metal lid from the jar ring and place it top side down inside the circle. Referring to Figure 4, pull the thread to gather the fabric edges tightly over the edge of the lid.

11. Cut a circle from the felt large enough to cover the gathering stitches and glue it to the bottom of the lid to finish as shown in Figure 5.

Figure 5

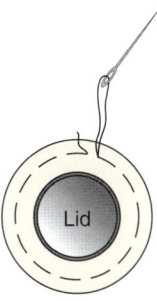

Figure 4

Sew Cozies Sew Jacket
Placement Diagram 12" x 4½"

AnniesCraftStore.com

Button Flower Jacket

Finished Size
Button Flower Jacket: 10" x 2½"

Materials
- Scrap red dot
- Scrap brown felt
- 1 fat eighth each ivory tonal and green dot
- 1 (3" x 10½") batting rectangle
- 1 (¾") red button
- 2 (⅝") red buttons
- Green No. 12 pearl cotton thread or embroidery floss
- 1 (3¼" tall x 12½" circumference) widemouthed glass canning jar with lid and ring
- 2½" length elastic cord
- ⅝" diameter cover button kit
- Fabric glue
- Thread
- Basic sewing tools and supplies

Cutting
Prepare pieces for fusible appliqué referring to Raw-Edge Fusible Appliqué on page 64.

From ivory tonal fat eighth:
- Cut 1 (3" x 10½") A rectangle.
- Cut 1 (3½" x 10½") B rectangle.

From green dot fat eighth:
- Cut 1 (1" x 10½") C strip.
- Cut 1 (4½") D circle.

Completing the Button Flower Jacket

1. Sew the C strip to one long side of the A rectangle to make an A-C unit; press seam toward C.

2. Referring to Figure 6, draw three straight lines up from C; one in the center about 1¼" tall and two about 1⅛" on each side, and about 1" tall. Transfer the leaf pattern to both sides of the center line and to the outer side of the other lines, as shown in the photo. Using one strand of pearl cotton or two strands of floss, sew a running stitch on the pattern lines.

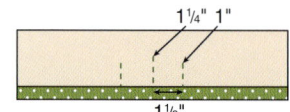

Figure 6

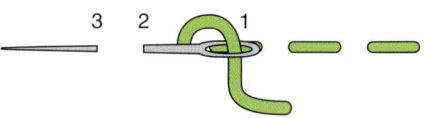

Running Stitch

3. Follow Steps 5–8 in the Sew Jacket directions to add the loop, batting and backing.

4. Sew the larger red button to the top of the center stem and the two smaller red buttons to the remaining stems.

5. Follow Steps 9–11 in the Sew Jacket directions to add the button closure and finish the lid.

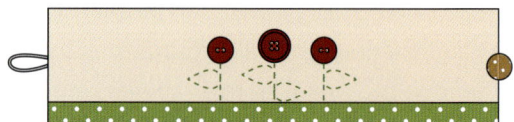

Sew Cozies Button Flower Jacket
Placement Diagram 10" x 2½"

Sew Cozies
Button Flower Jacket
Leaf Embroidery Pattern

Thread Jacket

Finished Size
Thread Jacket: 12½" x 2"

Materials
- Scraps brown and red tonal and tan dot
- Scrap brown felt
- Small piece red dot
- 1 fat eighth tan print
- 1 (2½" x 13") batting rectangle
- Cotton or polyester stuffing
- 2 each ¼" red and tan buttons
- 1 (3¼" tall x 12½" circumference) widemouthed glass canning jar with lid and ring
- Template material
- Fusible web with paper release
- 2½" length elastic cord
- ⅝" diameter cover button kit
- Fabric glue
- Thread
- Basic sewing tools and supplies

Cutting
Prepare pieces for fusible appliqué referring to Raw-Edge Fusible Appliqué on page 64.

From red dot:
- Cut 1 (6") circle.

From tan print:
- Cut 2 (2½" x 13") A rectangles.

Completing the Thread Jacket

1. Prepare templates for the thread and spool using the patterns provided.

2. Trace the patterns onto the paper side of the fusible web, cut the shapes apart and apply to the wrong side of the fabrics listed below. Cut out on pattern lines and remove the paper backing.

- Brown tonal: spool
- Red tonal: thread

3. Arrange the appliqués on the center of one of the A rectangles at an angle with the red shape covering the center of the spool. Fuse in place. Machine blanket-stitch around the appliqués using matching thread.

4. Follow Steps 5–8 in the Sew Jacket directions to add the loop and batting and backing.

5. Quilt around the edge of the appliqués and double-stitch a few loops with the red thread.

6. Sew the red and tan buttons near the thread loops as shown in the photo.

7. Follow Steps 8 and 9 in the Sew Jacket directions to add the button closure.

8. Follow Steps 10 and 11 in Sew Jacket directions, but insert stuffing in the center of the gathered circle before covering with the metal lid.

9. Place the pincushion lid on top of the jar and screw the lid down tightly, letting the pincushion pop through the top. ●

Here's a Tip
To use other size jars, measure the jar circumference and add ½" for the length of fabric strips and batting. Measure the jar height desired and add ½" for the width of fabric strip.

Sew Cozies Thread Jacket
Placement Diagram 12½" x 2"

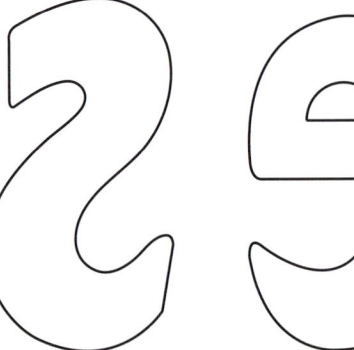
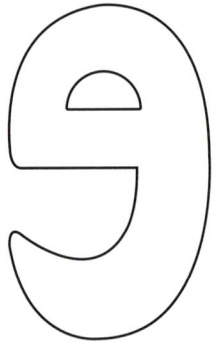
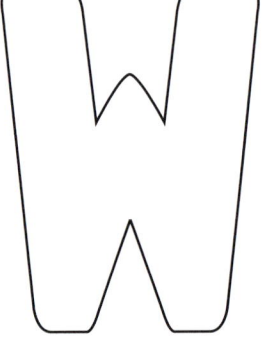

Sew Cozies
Spool
Cut as per instructions

Sew Cozies
Thread
Cut as per instructions

Sew Cozies
Sew Jacket Letters
Cut as per instructions

Sewing Machine Cover

Design by Chris Malone

This simple cover will keep your machine dust-free. It even has a little pocket in the front for supplies or the machine cord.

Skill Level
Beginner

Finished Size
Cover Size: 18" x 26", excluding ribbon ties

Materials
- Assorted scraps red, green, blue and gold dots and prints
- Small piece green dot
- ¼ yard red dot
- ½ yard tan tonal
- ½ yard cream text print
- ½ yard batting
- 60" length ⅞"-wide cream grosgrain ribbon
- Thread
- Basic sewing tools and supplies

Project Notes
Read all instructions before beginning this project.

Stitch right sides together using a ¼" seam allowance unless otherwise specified.

Materials and cutting lists assume 40" of usable fabric width for yardage.

Cutting

Measuring Your Machine
Note: Be sure to include any knobs or other features that extend out from the machine body when measuring.

1. Measure the width of your machine from side to side at the widest point. (W)

2. Measure the height of your machine from the bottom to the highest point. (H)

3. Measure the depth of your machine from the front to the back at the widest point. (D)

From assorted red, green, blue and gold scraps:
- Cut 16 (2½") D squares.

Note: If your measurement for the calculated length is lesser or greater than 26½", you may need to adjust the number of squares cut.

From green dot:
- Cut 1 (7" x 7½") pocket lining.
- Cut 1 (1" x 6½") E strip.
- Cut 2 (1" x 7") F strips.

From red dot:
- Cut 3 (2¼" by fabric width) binding strips.

From tan tonal:
Using the measurements taken for your machine, add H + D + H + ½" for length.

- Cut 1 (2½" x calculated length) A strip.
- Cut 1 (W less 4" x calculated length) B rectangle.

From cream text print:
- Cut 2 (2½" x 6½") C strips.
- Cut 1 (W + 2½") + (calculated length + 2") for lining.

From batting:
- Cut 1 rectangle the same size as the lining rectangle.
- Cut 1 (7" x 7½") pocket rectangle.

Completing the Cover

1. Arrange 13 D squares into one long row. Sew the squares together and press the seams open.

2. Sew the A strip and B rectangle on opposite sides of the D row as shown in Figure 1 to make an A-B-D unit; press seams toward A and B.

Note: If the D strip is longer than A and B, trim to fit.

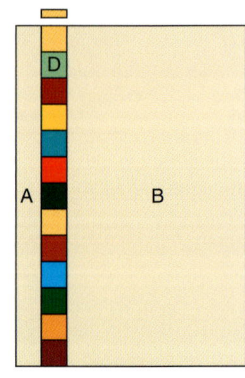

Figure 1

3. Layer the lining rectangle, batting rectangle and center the A-B-D unit, right side up. Baste layers together. Sample cover was quilted in-the-ditch of the two long seams, diagonal lines through the patchwork strip and vertical lines 2" apart across the cover. When quilting is complete, trim the backing and batting even with the cover front.

4. Sew the remaining three D squares together to make a row; press seams open.

5. Referring to Figure 2, sew C strips to each side of the D row to make a C-D unit; press seams toward C.

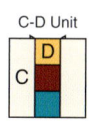

Figure 2

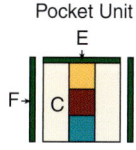

Figure 3

6. Sew the E strip to the top of the C-D unit as shown in Figure 3; press seam toward E. Sew F strips to opposite sides to complete the pocket unit; press seams toward F.

7. Layer and pin the pocket unit and the pocket lining, right sides facing, on the pocket batting. Stitch sides and top, leaving bottom open. Trim corners and trim batting close to the seam. Turn right side out and press. Referring to Figure 4, baste bottom edges together.

Figure 4

Figure 5

8. Referring to Figure 5, pin the pocket, right side up, on the bottom edge of the machine cover, 2½" from the right edge. Using matching thread, attach the pocket by stitching on the border seamline, backstitching at the top to hold the pocket securely.

9. Cut the ribbon into four 15" lengths. Measure 4½" from the bottom at each corner of the cover on the reverse side. Pin and baste a ribbon at each point as shown in Figure 6.

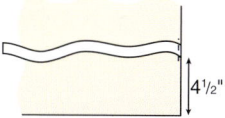

Figure 6

10. Refer to Quilting Basics on page 63 to bind the cover.

11. Place the cover over the machine and tie the ribbons in a bow at each side. ●

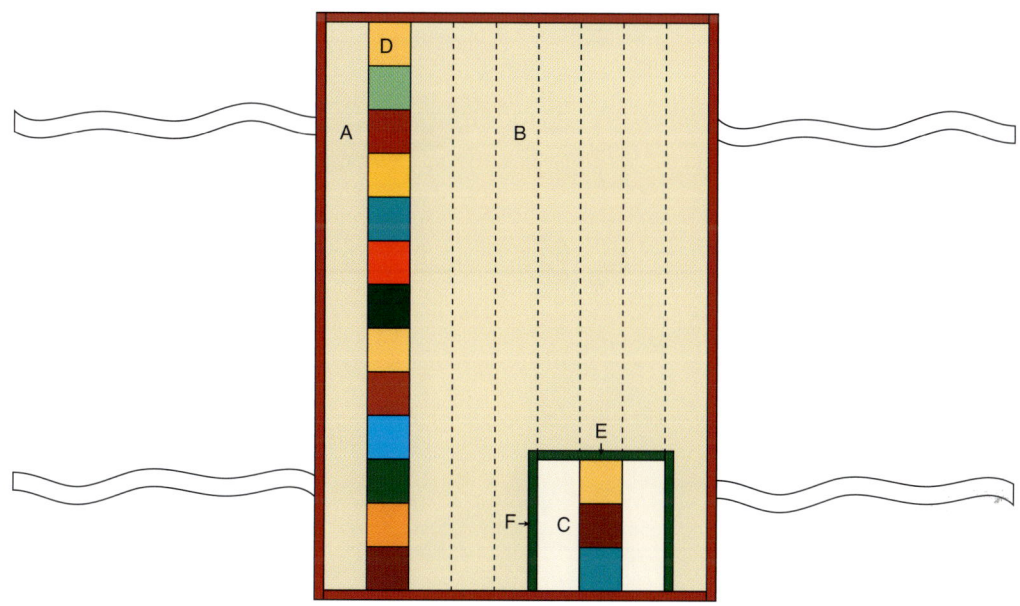

Sewing Machine Cover
Placement Diagram 18" x 26", excluding ribbon ties

Sewing Machine Organizer Pad

Design by Chris Malone

This pad, with its handy pockets and removable scrap basket, would be a great addition to your sewing room.

Skill Level
Beginner

Finished Sizes
Pad Size: 22" x 20"

Basket Size: 6" x 6" x 4"

Materials
- Scraps assorted red, green, blue and gold dots and prints
- ⅓ yard tan print
- ⅓ yard red dot
- ⅜ yard tan dot
- ⅔ yard ivory text print
- 22" x 24" backing rectangle
- ¾ yard batting
- 2 (8½" x 10½") fusible fleece
- 1 (1½") cover button kit
- Thread
- Basic sewing tools and supplies

Project Notes
Read all instructions before beginning this project.

Stitch right sides together using a ¼" seam allowance unless otherwise specified.

Materials and cutting lists assume 40" of usable fabric width for yardage.

Cutting

From scraps assorted red, green, blue and gold dots and prints:
- Cut 11 (2½") C squares.

From tan print:
- Cut 1 (8½" by fabric width) strip.
    Subcut strip into 2 (8½" x 10½") F and 1 (4½" x 14½") E rectangle.

From red dot:
- Cut 1 (8½" by fabric width) strip.
    Subcut strip into 2 (8½" x 10½") G rectangles and 1 (1¼" x 5") H strip.

From tan dot:
- Cut 1 (5½" by fabric width) strip.
    Subcut strip into 1 (5½" x 14½") D rectangle.
- Cut 3 (2¼" by fabric width) binding strips.

From ivory text print:
- Cut 1 (22½" x fabric width) strip.
    Subcut strip into 1 (12½" x 22½") A and 1 (6½" x 22½") B rectangle.

From batting:
- Cut 1 (22" x 24") rectangle.
- Cut 1 (5½" x 14½") rectangle.

Completing the Organizer Pad

1. Arrange and join the C squares into one long row; press seams open.

2. Sew an A rectangle to the top and a B rectangle to the bottom of the pieced C row to make an A-B-C unit as shown in Figure 1; press seams away from C.

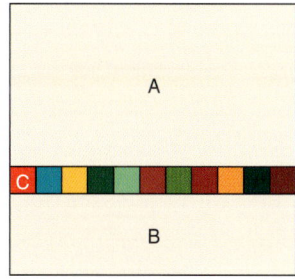

Figure 1

3. Layer the backing rectangle, right side down; same-size batting rectangle; and A-B-C unit, right side up. Baste layers together. Quilt in-the-ditch of the two long seams, quilt diagonal lines through the patchwork strip and quilt horizontal lines 2" apart across the pad (or quilt as desired). When quilting is complete, trim the backing and batting even with the pad top.

4. For the pocket, layer the D rectangle on the same-size batting piece, right side up, and top with the E rectangle, right side down, matching the raw edges on the top long side.

Note: *This will be the top of the pocket, so if you are using a directional print as used on the model, be sure it is going the correct direction.*

Stitch across the top long side through all layers as shown in Figure 2.

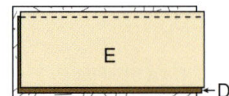

Figure 2

5. Trim batting close to the seam and referring to Figure 3, press E rectangle up with seam toward E. Refold E back down and match bottom raw edges, right sides facing, and stitch across the end on the left side.

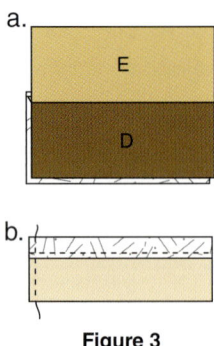

Figure 3

6. Trim corner and turn right side out; press well. Stitch-in-the-ditch of the seam line between D and E and baste the raw edges together as shown in Figure 4.

Figure 4

7. Referring to Figure 5, position the pocket at the bottom left corner of the pad, matching raw edges. Sew the right edge to the pad, stitching close to the seamed edge, and baste around the raw edges.

Decide what size pockets you would like (model has four evenly spaced sections) and stitch through all the layers, backstitching securely at the top edge to divide the pocket section.

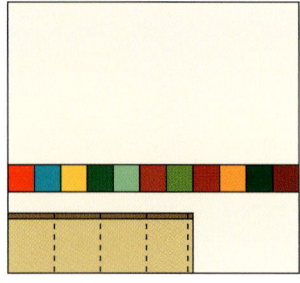

Figure 5

8. Referring to Quilting Basics on page 63, apply binding to complete the organizer pad.

Completing the Scrap Basket

1. Following manufacturer's directions, fuse the fleece rectangles to the wrong side of each F rectangle. Cut out a 2" x 2" square at the bottom corners of each F piece as shown in Figure 6.

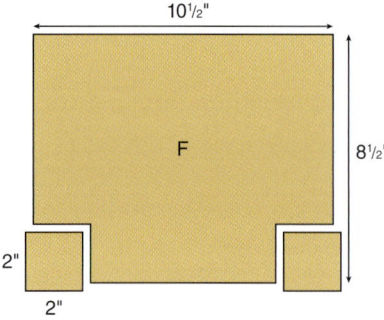

Figure 6

2. Referring to Figure 7, pin the F rectangles, right sides facing, and stitch the side and bottom seams; press seams open.

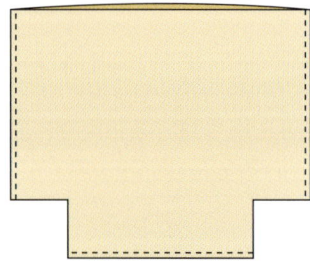

Figure 7

3. Fold the bottom seam to the adjacent side seam, matching seam lines, and stitch a ¼" seam as shown in Figure 8. Repeat on the other corner. Turn basket right side out.

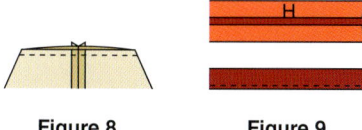

Figure 8   Figure 9

4. Referring to Figure 9, fold and press an H strip in half lengthwise, open and refold so the raw edges almost meet at the center crease. Press. Fold strip back in half again and topstitch the folded edges together.

5. Fold the hanging loop in half and pin the raw ends to the top center back of the basket as shown in Figure 10; machine-baste to hold.

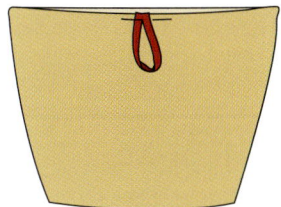

Figure 10

6. To make the basket lining, cut a 2" x 2" square out of the bottom corner of the two G rectangles. Sew the side and bottom seams as in Step 2 but leave a 4" opening on the bottom seam. Box the bottom corners as in Step 3. Do not turn right side out.

7. Slip the basket inside the lining (right sides together), matching the side seams, and pin and sew all around at the top. Turn the basket right side out through the opening in the bottom of the lining. Fold in the seam allowance on the lining opening and slip-stitch the folded edges together to close. Push the lining inside the basket and press the top edges flat.

8. Topstitch around the top of the basket ¼" from the edge.

9. Follow the manufacturer's directions to finish the cover button with one of the colored prints. Sew the button to the patchwork band as shown on the Placement Diagram and hang the scrap basket with the loop over the button. ●

Sewing Machine Pad
Placement Diagram 22" x 20"

Scrap Basket
Placement Diagram 6" x 6" x 4"

AnniesCraftStore.com

Ironing Board Caddy

Design by Chris Malone

This quick project is such a handy thing to have draped over the end of your ironing board. It has a removable pincushion for pins and needles and pockets on each end for storage.

Skill Level
Beginner

Finished Size
Caddy Size: 8½" x 36½"

Materials
- Scraps red, green, blue and gold dots and prints
- Small piece each green dot and red dot
- ⅓ yard ivory text print
- ½ yard tan dot
- Backing to size
- ½ yard batting
- 3½" length 1"-wide white hook-and-loop tape
- Small amount cotton or polyester stuffing
- Thread
- Basic sewing tools and supplies

Project Notes
Read all instructions before beginning this project.

Stitch right sides together using a ¼" seam allowance unless otherwise specified.

Materials and cutting lists assume 40" of usable fabric width for yardage.

Cutting

From scraps red, green, blue and gold dots and prints:
- Cut 8 (2") F squares.
- Cut 1 (3½" x 6½") pincushion back.

From green dot:
- Cut 1 (4" x 8½") E rectangle.

From red dot:
- Cut 1 (6½" x 8½") C rectangle.

From ivory text print:
- Cut 1 (8½" by fabric width) strip.
  Subcut strip into 1 (8½" x 36½") A rectangle.

From tan dot:
- Cut 1 (7½" by fabric width) strip.
  Subcut strip into 1 (7½" x 8½") B and 1 (5" x 8½") D rectangle.
- Cut 3 (2½" by fabric width) binding strips.

From batting:
- Cut 1 (8½" x 36½") rectangle for caddy.
- Cut 1 (8½" x 7½") rectangle for large pocket.
- Cut 1 (8½" x 5") rectangle for small pocket.
- Cut 3 (3½" x 6½") rectangles for pincushion.

Completing the Caddy

1. Layer backing, right side down, batting and the A rectangle, right side up, matching raw edges. Pin- or thread-baste and quilt three vertical lines evenly spaced across the rectangle, or quilt as desired, to secure the layers.

2. Layer the B rectangle on a same-size batting piece, right side up, and top with the C rectangle, right side down, matching the raw edges at one end. Stitch across at that end through all layers as shown in Figure 1.

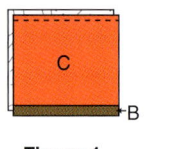 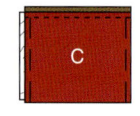

Figure 1   Figure 2

3. Trim the batting close to the seam. Referring to Figure 2, flip C right side up, matching raw edges at the bottom, creating a B band at the top front. The wrong sides of the two fabrics are now facing and the batting is sandwiched in the middle. Stitch-in-the-ditch of the seam line and baste the raw edges together to complete the Large Pocket Unit.

4. Repeat Step 3 using the D rectangle, same-size batting rectangle and E rectangle to make a Small Pocket Unit.

5. Position a pocket on each end of the caddy, right sides up. Baste to hold. Divide the pockets by stitching down the center of each one, backstitching securely at the top edge as shown in Figure 3.

Figure 3

6. Refer to Quilting Basics on page 63 to bind the caddy.

7. Referring to Figure 4, arrange and sew the F squares into two rows of four squares each; press. Join the rows together to complete the pincushion top; press.

Pincushion Top

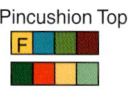

Figure 4

8. Baste the same-size batting rectangle to the wrong side of the pincushion top and stitch-in-the-ditch or quilt as desired.

9. Position the hook side of the hook-and-loop strip on the center of the back and stitch around the edges to attach as shown in Figure 5.

Figure 5

10. Pin the pincushion top and back together, right sides facing, and stitch all round, leaving a 3" opening on one long side. Trim the corners and turn right side out. Stuff the pincushion firmly. Fold in the seam allowance on the opening and whipstitch the folded edges together to close.

11. Determine preferred placement of the pincushion.

Note: It is placed about 5" above the large pocket on the model, which will place it at the front edge of the ironing board if the large pockets are in front.

12. Position the loop side of the hook-and-loop tape on the caddy in the desired place and stitch around the edges to hold. Attach the pincushion to finish. ●

Ironing Board Caddy
Placement Diagram 8½" x 36½"

Thread Spools Pincushion

Design by Kathleen Berlew

This easy hand-sewing design is a great stash-busting project and will make a cheery addition to your sewing room.

Skill Level
Beginner

Finished Size
Pincushion Size: 6" x 7"

Materials
- Scraps bright blue, light aqua, bright pink, chartreuse, red orange, green, orange and yellow wool felt*
- 3" x 6" beige wool felt*
- 3" x 6" champagne wool felt*
- 6" x 7" camel wool felt*
- 6" x 8" fuchsia wool felt*
- Fat eighth off-white wool felt*
- Dark coral, cranberry, Kelly green, plum, light topaz, medium tangerine, very light sky blue, light beige brown, light parrot green, dark yellow beige, very light desert sand, straw and medium bright turquoise embroidery floss
- Tissue or tracing paper
- Black fine-point permanent marker
- 4 cups ground walnut shells
- Thread
- Basic sewing tools and supplies

National Nonwovens wool felt used to make sample.

Project Notes
Read all instructions before beginning this project.

Stitch right sides together using a ¼" seam allowance unless otherwise specified.

Cutting
Prepare template using patterns provided.

From scraps each bright blue, light aqua, bright pink, chartreuse, red orange, green, orange and yellow wool felt:
- Cut 1 (1 x 1⅛") small spool thread piece.

From beige wool felt:
- Cut 3 small spools.

From champagne wool felt:
- Cut 3 small spools.

From camel wool felt:
- Cut 1 large spool and 3 small spools.

From fuchsia wool felt:
- Cut 1 large thread piece and 1 (1 x 1⅛") small spool thread piece.

From off-white wool felt:
- Cut 2 (6½" x 8") for A front and B back rectangles.

Completing the Pincushion

1. Trace dash lines from embroidery template onto tissue paper with marker. Pin tissue paper onto A rectangle. Use two strands of floss and backstitch to embroider lines, sewing through felt and tissue paper as follows: Use cranberry floss for right border, dark coral for bottom border, Kelly green for left border and medium bright turquoise for top border. When stitching is complete, gently tear tissue paper away from stitches. Use tweezers, if necessary, to remove small bits of paper.

2. Referring to Placement Diagram, arrange small spools on A and pin in place. Use two strands of floss and backstitch to sew spools in place, sewing approximately 1/16" from edge, as follows: Use light beige brown floss for camel spools, dark yellow beige floss for beige spools and very light desert sand floss for champagne spools.

3. Referring to Placement Diagram, arrange small spool thread pieces on top of spools. Sew in place with matching embroidery floss, using backstitch on top and bottom edges, and whipstitch on side edges. Embroider five backstitch lines evenly spaced across each spool.

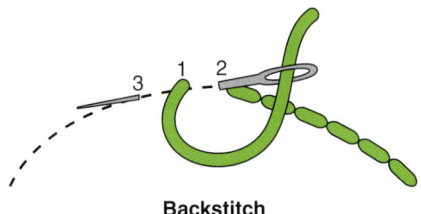

Backstitch

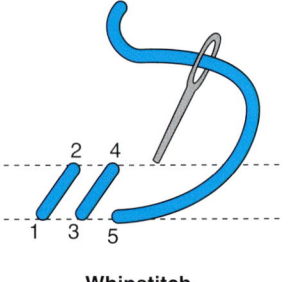

Whipstitch

Tip: Use a piece of painter's tape as a guide for sewing straight lines. It can be repositioned several times and should release easily from the felt surface.

4. Pin large spool, centered, on B rectangle. Sew in place with two strands of light beige brown floss and backstitch, sewing approximately 1/16" from edges.

5. Trace dash lines from large thread embroidery template onto tissue paper with permanent marker and pin onto fuchsia large thread piece. With two strands of plum floss, backstitch lines, sewing through felt and tissue paper. When stitching is complete, gently tear tissue paper away, as above.

6. Fold embroidered fuchsia piece in half widthwise, wrong sides together, and press fold with hot iron to make sharp crease. Pin folded piece on top of large spool to make pocket (folded edge will be at top of spool). With plum floss and backstitch, sew pocket in place, sewing through all layers approximately 1/16" from side and bottom edges.

7. Pin front and back of pincushion together, right sides facing, and sew pieces together with matching sewing thread and ¼" seam. Leave opening at bottom for turning.

8. Trim seams and clip corners. Turn pincushion to right side and fill firmly with ground walnut shells. Sew opening closed. ●

Thread Spools Pincushion
Placement Diagram 6" x 7"

Thread Spools Pincushion
Large Thread Embroidery Template

Fold Line

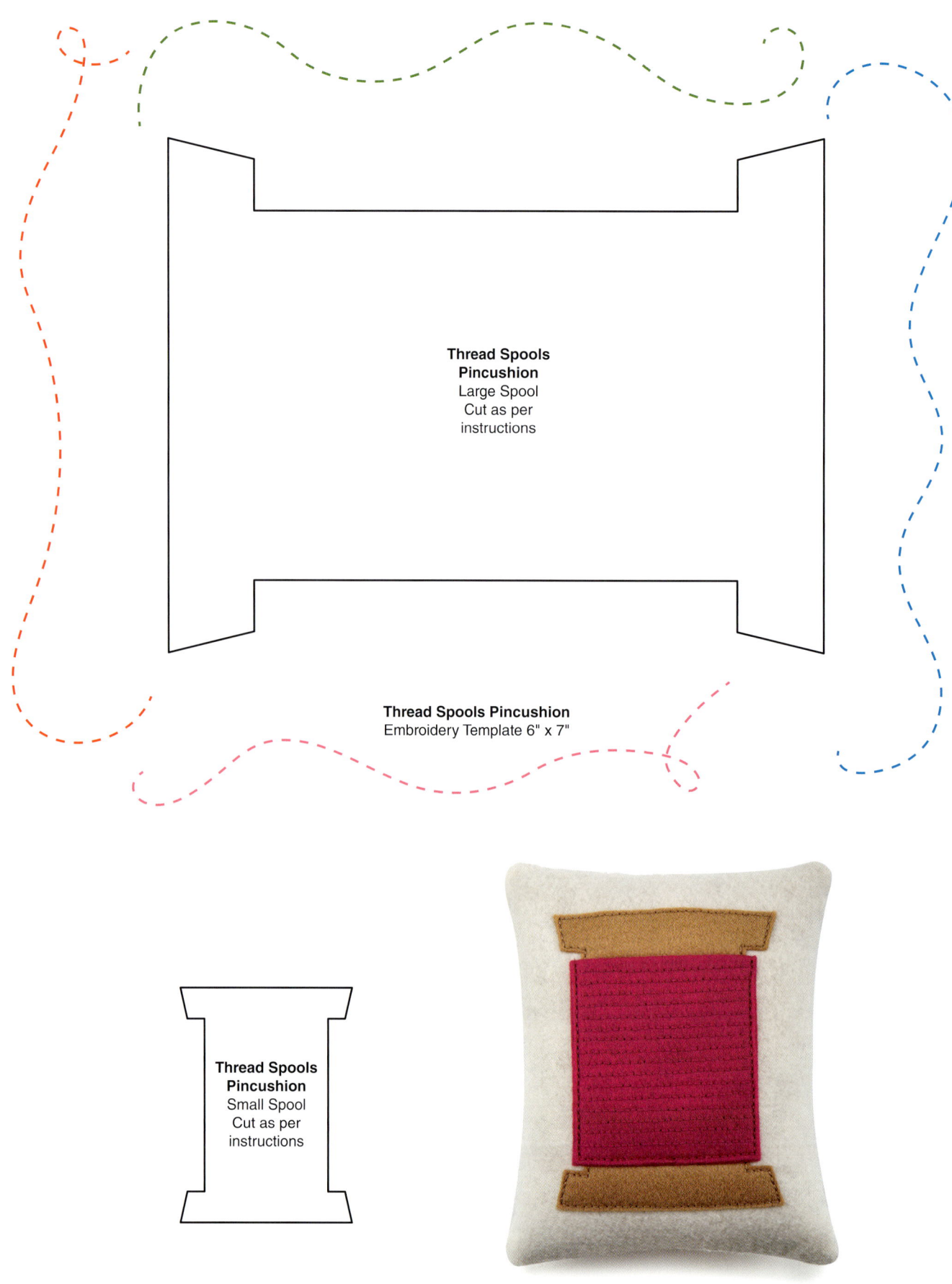

Thread Spools Pincushion
Large Spool
Cut as per instructions

Thread Spools Pincushion
Embroidery Template 6" x 7"

Thread Spools Pincushion
Small Spool
Cut as per instructions

Tricolor Table Topper

Designed & Quilted by Cathey Laird of Cathey Marie Designs

This is a project with a homey touch. It can be made into a holiday or seasonal topper just by changing the fabrics.

Skill Level
Beginner

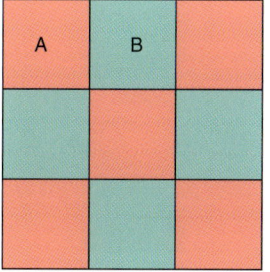

Nine-Patch
6" x 6" Finished Block
Make 4

Finished Sizes
Quilt Size: 23" x 23"

Block Size: 6" x 6"

Number of Blocks: 4

Materials
- ⅓ yard multicolored floral print*
- ⅓ yard white print*
- ½ yard green print*
- Backing to size
- Batting to size*
- Thread*
- Basic sewing tools and supplies

*Sunnyside Up collection from Moda; batting from The Warm Company and Aurifil thread used to make sample.

Project Notes
Read all instructions before beginning this project.

Stitch right sides together using a ¼" seam allowance unless otherwise specified.

Materials and cutting lists assume 40" of usable fabric width for yardage.

Cutting

From multicolored floral print:
- Cut 4 (2½" by fabric width) strips.
  Subcut strips into 4 (2½" x 13") A strips, 2 (2½" x 19½") H strips and 2 (2½" x 23½") I strips.

From white print:
- Cut 1 (9¾" by fabric width) strip.
  Subcut strip into 1 (6½") C square, 1 (9¾") D square and 2 (5⅛") E squares. Cut D square on both diagonals to make 4 D triangles and cut E squares in half on 1 diagonal to make 4 E triangles.

From green print:
- Cut 2 (2½" by fabric width) strips.
  Subcut strips into 4 (2½" x 13") B strips.
- Cut 2 (1½" by fabric width) strips.
  Subcut strips into 2 (1½" x 17½") F and 2 (1½" x 19½") G strips.
- Cut 3 (2½" by fabric width) binding strips.

Completing the Blocks

1. Sew B strips on opposite sides of an A strip to make a B-A-B strip set as shown in Figure 1; press. Subcut strip set into 4 (2½" x 6½") B-A-B units.

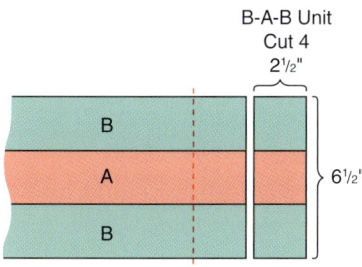

Figure 1

2. Referring to Figure 2, sew A strips on opposite sides of a B strip to make an A-B-A strip set; press. Repeat to make a second A-B-A strip set. Subcut strip sets into 8 (2½" x 6½") A-B-A units.

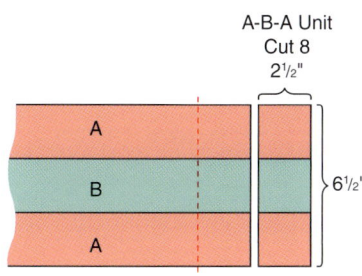

Figure 2

3. Join two A-B-A units and one B-A-B unit as shown in Figure 3 to make a Nine-Patch block; press. Repeat to make a total of four Nine-Patch blocks.

Figure 3

Completing the Topper

Refer to the Assembly Diagram and project photo for orientation and placement of borders.

1. Arrange and stitch Nine-Patch blocks, C square and D and E triangles into diagonal rows; press.

2. Join rows together to complete the quilt top center; press.

3. Sew F strips to opposite sides of the top center and G strips to the top and bottom; press.

4. Sew H strips to opposite sides and I strips to the top and bottom to complete the quilt top; press.

5. Create a quilt sandwich referring to Quilting Basics on page 63.

6. Quilt as desired. The sample quilt was machine-quilted with an edge-to-edge floral loop design.

7. Join the binding strips and bind the edges referring to Quilting Basics on page 63. ●

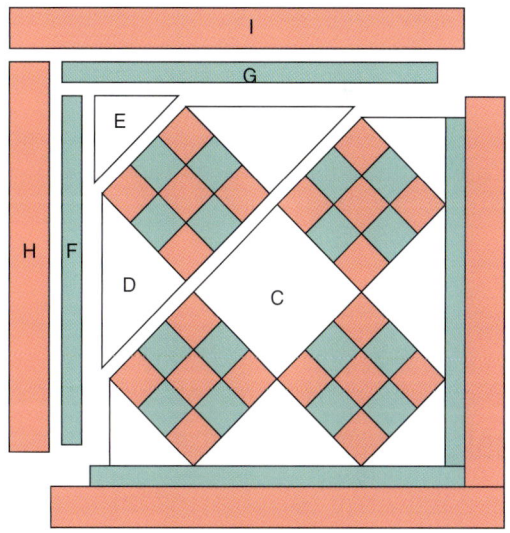

Tricolor Table Topper
Assembly Diagram 23" x 23"

Daisy Fields Table Set

Designed & Quilted by Chris Malone

Set a cheerful table with these pieced and appliquéd pieces. Quilted scallops add a little zest to the design!

Skill Level
Beginner

Table Runner

Finished Size
Table Runner Size: 12" x 52", including scallops

Materials
- Scrap yellow tonal
- Small pieces each 4 green tonals/prints
- Small pieces white tonal
- Fat eighth each 4 red tonals/prints
- Fat eighth each 4 gray tonals/prints
- 12½" x 48½" backing
- 12½" x 48½" batting plus scraps
- Fusible web with paper release
- Template Material
- Thread
- Basic sewing tools and supplies

Cutting

From each red tonal/print fat eighth:
- Cut 8 (3½") squares for a total of 32 A squares.

From each gray tonal/print fat eighth:
- Cut 8 (3½") squares for a total of 32 B squares.

Completing the Runner

1. Arrange four different A squares into two rows. Sew squares together into rows and join rows together to make one A Four-Patch unit as shown in Figure 1; press. Repeat with the remaining A squares to make a total of 8 identical units.

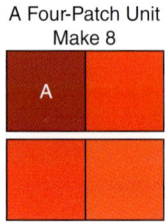

A Four-Patch Unit
Make 8

Figure 1

2. Referring to Figure 2, repeat Step 1 using the B squares to make a total of 8 B Four-Patch units.

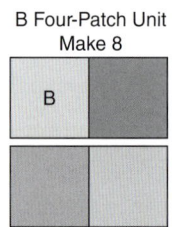

B Four-Patch Unit
Make 8

Figure 2

3. Prepare a daisy and daisy center template using the patterns provided.

4. Referring to Raw-Edge Fusible Appliqué on page 64, draw the daisy and daisy center pattern eight times each on the paper side of the fusible web. Apply the fusible web to the wrong side of the appliquéd fabrics as listed below. Cut out the shapes on the pattern lines and remove the paper backing.

- White tonal: 8 daisies
- Yellow tonal: 8 daisy centers

5. Center a daisy and daisy center on each of the A Four-Patch units and fuse in place as shown in Figure 3. Machine blanket-stitch around the appliqués using matching thread.

Make 8

Figure 3

6. Alternately arrange the A and B Four-Patch units into two rows of eight units each. Sew the blocks together in each row; press. Sew the rows together to complete the runner top; press.

7. Prepare the scallop template using the pattern provided. Trace the pattern two times on the wrong side of each of the four green fabrics. Referring to Figure 4, fold the fabrics in half with right sides facing and pattern on top and pin to batting scraps. Sew all around on pattern lines, leaving open at the straight edge. Cut out ⅛" from the seam, trim the batting close to the seam and clip the curves. Turn right side out and press edges flat. Topstitch ¼" from edge. Repeat to make a total of eight scallops.

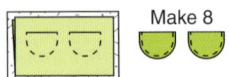

Make 8

Figure 4

8. Arrange four scallops on each short end of the table runner, matching the straight raw edges and placing the end scallops about ⅜" from the edge as shown in Figure 5. Baste to hold.

Figure 5

9. Referring to Figure 6, layer the batting; backing, right side up; and runner top, right side down; and pin to hold. Sew all around, leaving a 6" opening on one long side. Trim the corners and turn right side out, pulling the scallops outward. Press the edges flat. Fold in the seam allowance on the opening and slip-stitch the folded edges together to close.

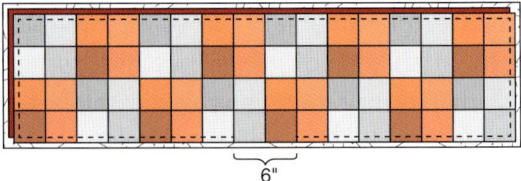

Figure 6

10. Topstitch ¼" from the edge and baste the center layers with thread or pins to hold. Quilt as desired to finish. Sample quilt was stitched-in-the-ditch between units with appliqués quilted around each motif and a matching flower motif quilted in each B Four-Patch unit.

Daisy Fields Table Runner
Placement Diagram 12" x 52", including scallops

Place Mat

Finished Size
Place Mat Size: 17" x 12", including scallops

Materials
Materials listed make one place mat.
- Small pieces each 4 green tonals/prints
- Small pieces each 4 red tonals/prints
- 1 (12½") D square gray print
- 12½" x 15½" backing
- 12½" x 15½" batting plus scraps
- Thread
- Basic sewing tools and supplies

Cutting

From each red tonal/print:
- Cut 4 (2") squares for a total of 16 C squares.

Completing the Place Mat

1. Arrange the C squares into two rows of eight squares each as shown in Figure 7. Sew the squares into rows and the rows together to make a C unit; press.

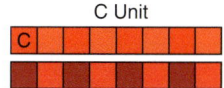
Figure 7

2. Referring to Figure 8, join the C unit to one side of the D square to make the place mat top; press.

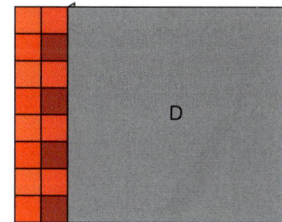
Figure 8

3. Follow Step 7 in the Table Runner instructions to make four scallops, one each from the green fabrics.

4. Arrange the scallops as shown in Figure 9, matching raw edges and with the end scallops ⅜" from the edge of the place mat. Baste to hold.

Figure 9

5. Follow Steps 9 and 10 in the Table Runner instructions to assemble and finish the place mat.

Daisy Fields Place Mat
Placement Diagram 17" x 12", including scallops

Coaster

Finished Size
Coaster Size: 8" x 6", including scallops

Materials
Materials listed make one coaster.
- Scrap yellow tonal
- Scrap white tonal
- Small pieces each 2 green tonals/prints
- Small pieces each 4 red tonals/prints
- 6½" x 6½" backing
- 2 (6½" x 6½") batting squares plus scraps
- Fusible web with paper release
- Template material
- Thread
- Basic sewing tools and supplies

Cutting

From each red tonal/print:
- Cut 4 (3½") E squares.

Completing the Coaster

1. Arrange and sew the four E squares into two rows; press. Sew the rows together to complete the coaster top.

2. Baste one of the batting squares to the wrong side of the coaster top.

3. Follow Steps 3–5 in the Table Runner instructions to make a flower appliqué centered on the coaster top.

4. Follow Step 7 in the Table Runner instructions to make two green scallops.

5. Arrange the two scallops on one side of the appliquéd coaster top, matching raw edges and with the scallops ⅜" from the corners. Baste to hold.

6. Place the backing, right side up, on the remaining batting square and cover with the coaster front, right side down; pin. Sew all around, leaving a 4" opening on a side without the scallops. Trim the corners and trim one of the batting squares close to the seam to reduce the bulk. Turn right side out, pulling the scallops outward. Press the edges flat. Fold in the seam allowance on the opening and slip-stitch the folded edges together to close.

7. Topstitch ¼" from the edges and quilt as desired to finish. ●

Daisy Fields Coaster
Placement Diagram 8" x 6", including scallops

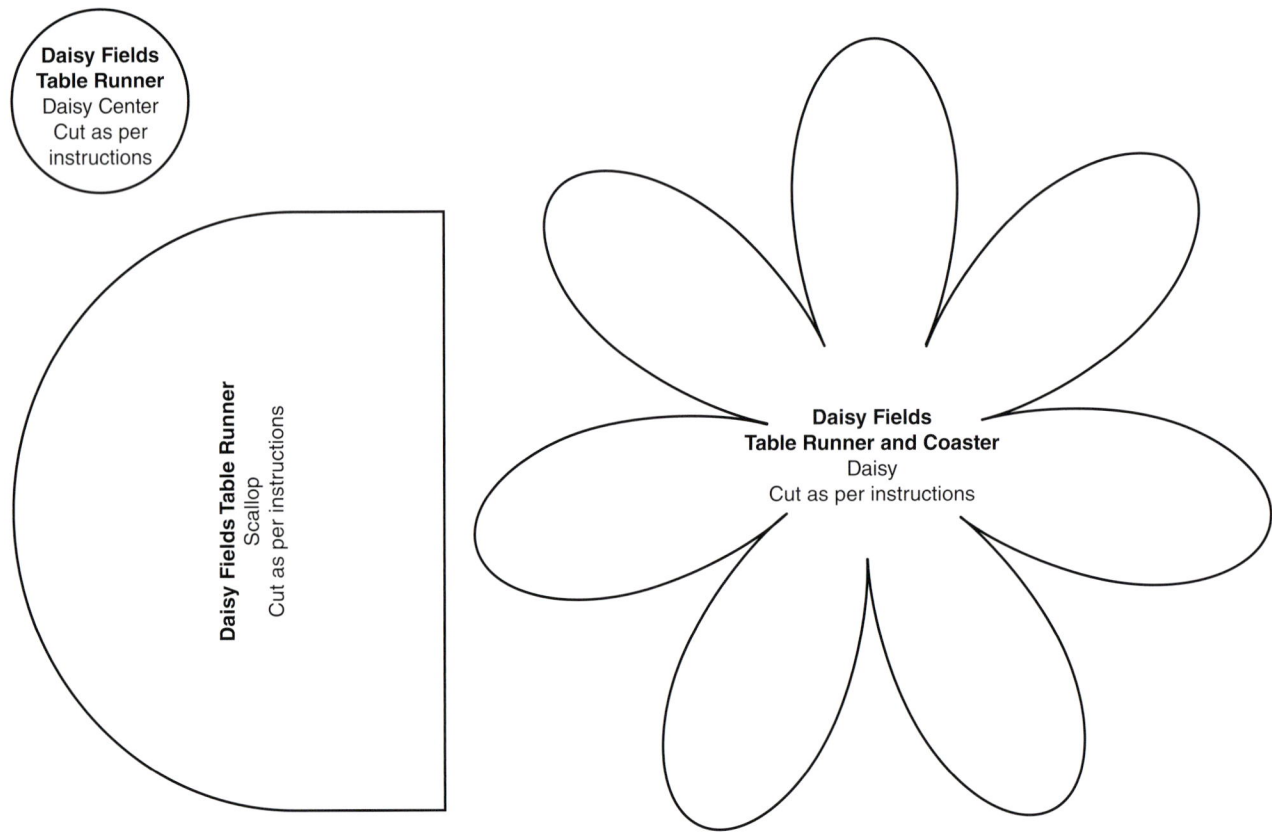

AnniesCraftStore.com

Summer Fun Mug Rugs

Designed & Quilted by Bev Getschel

Use your favorite fabric scraps to make this smiling duo in an afternoon.

Skill Level
Confident Beginner

Lady Bug Mug Rug

Finished Size
Mug Rug Size: 12" x 7½"

Materials
Materials listed make one Lady Bug Mug Rug.
- Scraps white solid*
- 8" x 8" piece red tonal*
- 9" x 10" ivory-with-gold dot A rectangle*
- Fat eighth black solid*
- 9" x 13" backing*
- 9" x 13" batting*
- Black felt for the legs and antennae
- Fusible web with paper release*
- Black permanent marker
- Template material
- Thread
- Basic sewing tools and supplies

*Fabric from Hoffman California-International Fabrics, batting from Fairfield and fusible web from HeatnBond used to make sample.

Cutting
Prepare templates using provided patterns.

From scraps white solid:
- Cut 2 eyes.

From red tonal:
- Cut 1 body and 1 body reversed.

From black solid:
- Cut 1 head.
- Cut 1 abdomen.

From black felt:
- Cut 2 Leg No. 1.
- Cut 2 Leg No. 2.
- Cut 2 Leg No. 3.
- Cut 2 Antennae.

Completing the Mug Rug

1. Join red bodies on opposite sides of the black abdomen as shown in Figure 1; press. Sew head to the body-abdomen unit; press.

Figure 1

2. Referring to Raw-Edge Fusible Appliqué on page 64, trace two large spots and four small spots on the paper side of the fusible web. Cut around each shape and fuse on the wrong side of black solid scraps. Cut on drawn line and fuse on the body sections referring to Placement Diagram. Machine-stitch with matching thread to secure.

3. Turn under ¼" on right edge of the lady bug. Referring to Figure 2, position the bug on A rectangle and tuck one each Leg No. 1, No. 2 and No. 3 in place. Hand-stitch or machine zigzag-stitch folded edge to A, catching legs to secure.

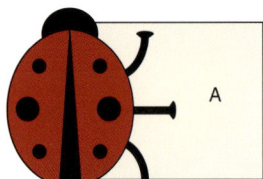

Figure 2

4. With raw edges aligned, machine-baste remaining three legs and two antennae to the lady bug top.

5. Layer batting, quilt back right side up, and quilt top right side down, as shown in Figure 3. Stitch around all sides leaving a 4" opening on bottom long edge.

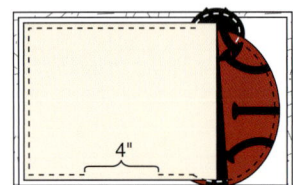

Figure 3

6. Trim batting close to the stitching, clip corners and turn right side out; press. Fold seam allowances in and whipstitch opening closed.

7. Using a black marker, draw pupils on the white eyes and machine-stitch to the head to finish. Sample mug rug was machine-quilted with a free motion loop pattern in an A rectangle.

Summer Fun Mug Rugs
Lady Bug
Placement Diagram 12" x 7½"

Shining Sun Mug Rug

Finished Size
Mug Rug Size: 12" x 7½"

Materials
Materials listed make one Shining Sun Mug Rug.
- Scraps white and black solid*
- Fat eighth yellow solid*
- Fat quarter white-with-black dot*
- 8" x 11½" batting*
- Fusible web with paper release*
- Template material
- Thread
- Basic sewing tools and supplies

*ME + YOU fabric from Hoffman California-International Fabrics, Batting from Fairfield and fusible web from HeatnBond used to make sample.

Cutting
Prepare templates using provided patterns.

From yellow solid:
- Cut 10 petals and 10 petals reversed.
- Cut 1 sun.

From white-with-black dot:
- Cut 2 (8" x 11½") B rectangles.

Completing the Mug Rug
1. Draw a 4½" circle on the wrong side of one B rectangle as shown in Figure 4. Extend the drawn line on a gentle curve to the top and bottom edges of B.

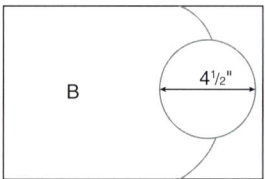

Figure 4

2. Referring to Figure 5, layer batting, one B rectangle right side up, and remaining B rectangle with drawn lines right side down. Stitch ¼" from edge on straight sides and following the drawn lines on one end, leaving a 4" opening on opposite end. Trim corners, clip curves and turn right side out; press. Turn under seam allowances and whipstitch closed.

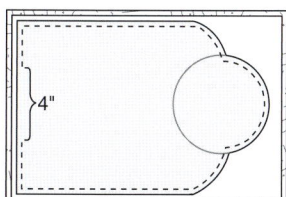

Figure 5

3. Pair one petal and one petal reversed and stitch on two sides, leaving the bottom open as shown in Figure 6. Clip curves, turn and press. Repeat to make a total of 10 petals.

Figure 6

4. Referring to Figure 7, draw a 4½" circle on the right side of the mug rug.

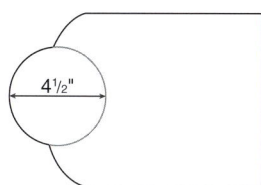

Figure 7

5. Position petals ¼" over drawn line, overlapping as needed as shown in Figure 8 to fill the circle with petals. Stitch petals in place.

Figure 8

6. Referring to Raw-Edge Fusible Appliqué on page 64, draw a 4½" circle on the paper side of fusible web. Cut around circle, remove paper and iron on the wrong side of yellow solid. Cut on drawn line and fuse in place covering the raw edges of the petals. Machine zigzag-stitch using matching thread to secure the sun.

7. Repeat Step 6, preparing two eyes from white solid and two eyeballs and one smile from black solid. Layer and fuse eyeballs on eyes and fuse on the sun. Fuse the smile in place. Machine zigzag-stitch using matching thread around each appliqué shape.

8. Quilt with straight lines radiating out from the sun. ●

Summer Fun Mug Rugs
Shining Sun
Placement Diagram 12" x 7½"

AnniesCraftStore.com

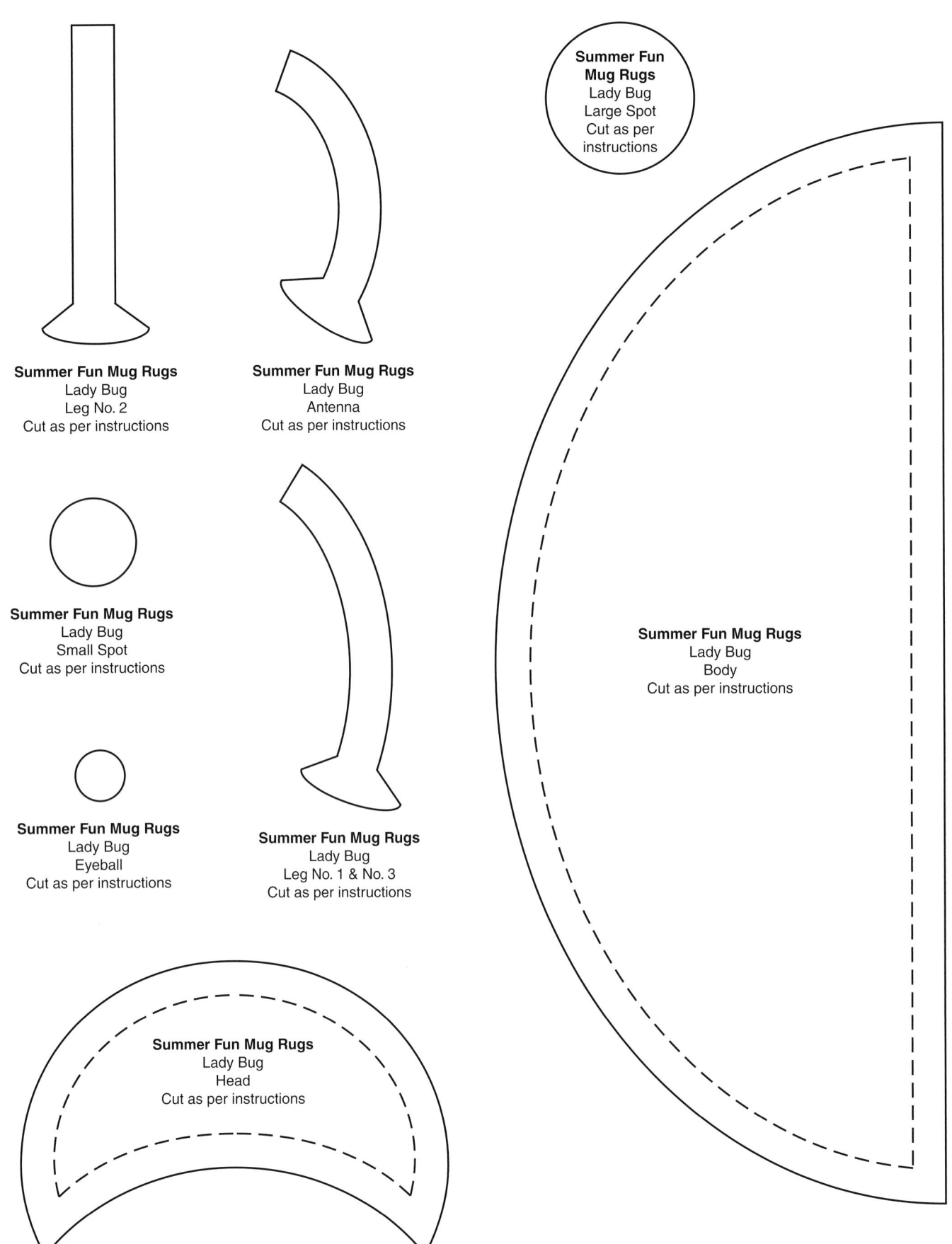

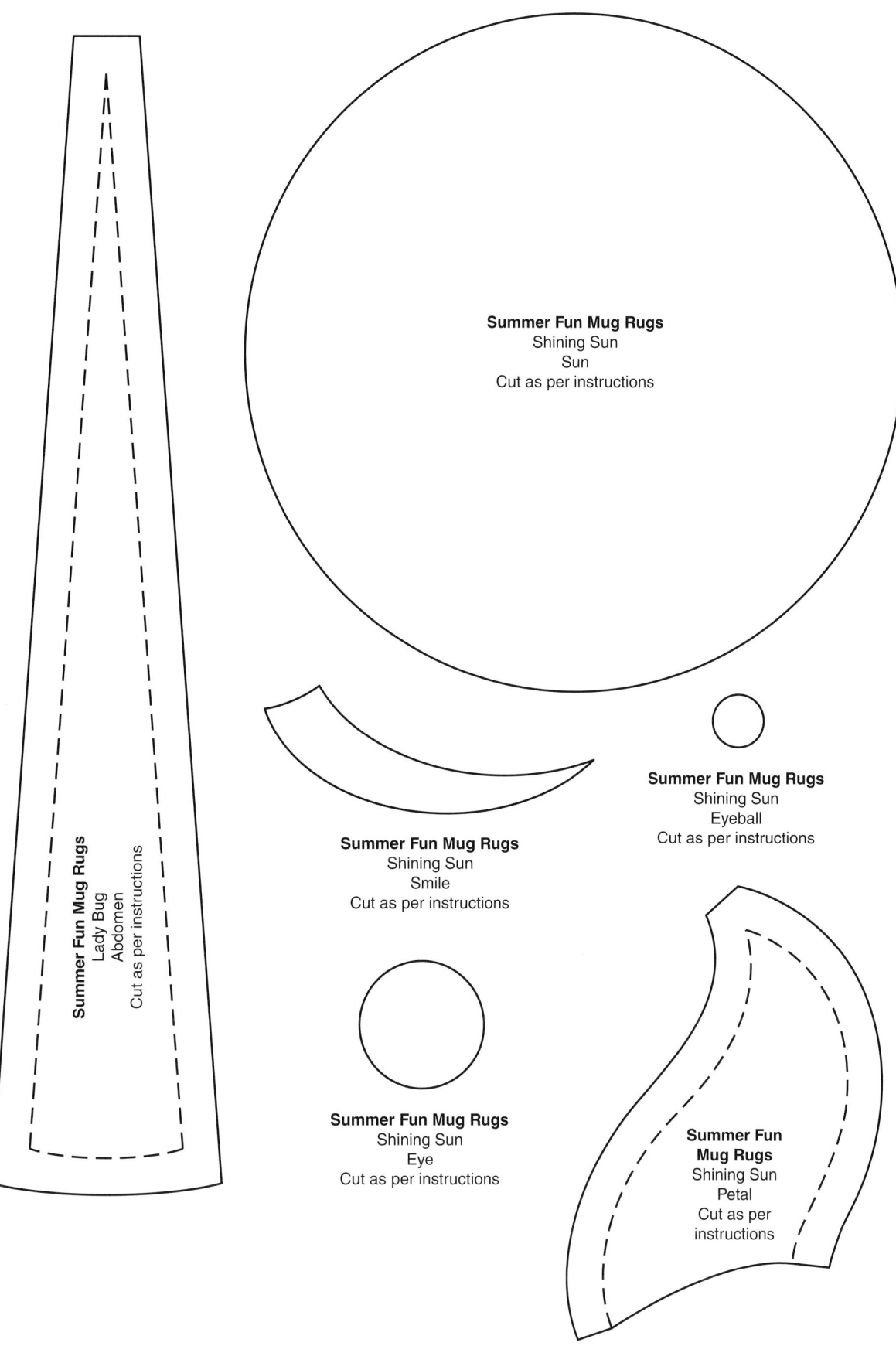

Bright Blocks Pot Holders

Designed & Quilted by Chris Malone

Grab the scrap bin and whip up a few bright pot holders for the kitchen. A set makes a thoughtful gift because these are so practical and decorative.

Skill Level:
Beginner

Finished Size
Pot Holder Size: 8" x 8"

MAKE IN A DAY

Materials
Materials listed make one set of three pot holders—one in each pattern.

- Scraps assorted bright-color solids, tonals and prints
- ⅓ yard dark gray tonal
- ⅓ yard black-with-multicolored dots
- 3 (8") backing squares
- 3 (8") cotton batting squares
- 3 (8") needlepunch insulated batting squares
- Thread
- Basic sewing tools and supplies

Project Notes
Read all instructions before beginning this project.

Stitch right sides together using a ¼" seam allowance unless otherwise specified.

Materials and cutting lists assume 40" of usable fabric width for yardage.

Cutting

From assorted bright-color solids, tonals and prints:
- Cut 33 (2") D squares.

From dark gray tonal:
- Cut 1 (8½" by fabric width) strip.
  Subcut strip into 1 (8½") A square, 1 (5") C square and 4 (3½") B squares.
  Subcut the A square in half on 1 diagonal to make 2 A triangles.

From black-with-multicolored dots:
- Cut 3 (2¼" by fabric width) binding strips.
- Cut 1 (1¼" by fabric width) strip.
  Subcut strip into 3 (1¼" x 5½") hanging loop strips.

Completing the Pot Holder Tops

Diagonal Stripe Pot Holder
1. Arrange and sew eight D squares in a row as shown in Figure 1 to make a D unit; press.

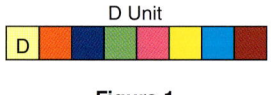

D Unit

Figure 1

2. Referring to Figure 2, center and stitch an A triangle on each side of the D unit; press seams toward A.

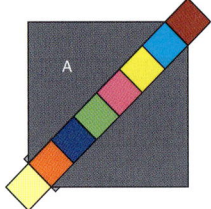

Figure 2

3. Trim the top to 8" square, centering the ruler so an even amount is trimmed off each side, to complete the pot holder top.

Bright Blocks Pot Holders
Diagonal Stripe Pot Holder
Placement Diagram 8" x 8"

Cross Stripe Pot Holder

1. Arrange and sew five D squares in a row as shown in Figure 3 to make a D unit; press.

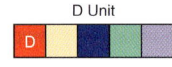

Figure 3

2. Arrange and stitch two D squares together to make a two-patch unit; press. Referring to Figure 4, sew a B square to each side of the two-patch unit to make a B-D unit; press seams toward B. Repeat to make a second B-D unit.

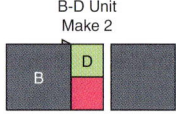

Figure 4

3. Sew the D unit between the two B-D units to complete the pot holder top; press seams toward the B-D units.

Bright Blocks Pot Holders
Cross Stripe Pot Holder
Placement Diagram 8" x 8"

Bordered Pot Holder

1. Arrange and sew D squares into two rows of five squares each and two rows of three squares each as shown in Figure 5; press.

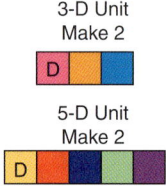

Figure 5

AnniesCraftStore.com

2. Sew 3-D units to each side of C to make a C-D unit; press seams toward C.

3. Referring to Figure 6, sew the 5-D strips to the top and bottom of the C-D unit to complete the pot holder top; press seams toward the C-D unit.

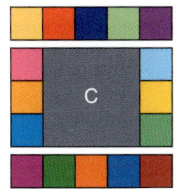

Figure 6

Bright Blocks Pot Holders
Bordered Pot Holder
Placement Diagram 8" x 8"

Finishing the Pot Holders

1. Layer the backing square, right side down; insulated batting; cotton batting; and one pieced top, right side up. Baste layers together and quilt straight lines ½" apart, or as desired. Repeat with remaining backings, battings and tops.

2. Fold and press each hanging loop strip in half lengthwise; open and refold so the raw edges almost meet at the center crease as shown in Figure 7; press.

Figure 7

3. Fold strips back in half again and topstitch the folded edges together, again referring to Figure 7.

4. Referring to Figure 8, pin the raw edges of the hanging loop on one corner of each pot holder back, about ¾" from the corner. Baste in place.

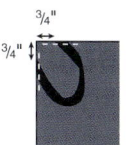

Figure 8

5. Referring to Quilting Basics on page 63, bind the edges of each pot holder with the strips to complete the pot holders. ●

Microwave Cozies

Design by Chris Malone

These handy cozies are perfect for heating up a mug of coffee, a bowl of soup or even a serving dish of food, and removing them from the microwave safely and comfortably.

Skill Level
Beginner

Finished Sizes
Small Cozy Size: 6¼" x 6¼" x 2"
Medium Cozy Size: 8¼" x 8¼" x 2"
Large Cozy Size: 12¼" x 12¼" x 2"

MAKE IN A DAY

Materials
Materials listed make one set of three cozies—small, medium and large.

- ⅛ yard each orange and blue dot
- ¼ yard pink dot
- ½ yard each butterfly print and black-with-white dot
- Cotton batting
- Cotton thread
- Basic sewing tools and supplies

Note: *It is important to use only 100% cotton fabric, batting and thread for these cozies, because polyester may melt in the microwave and materials with metallic fibers can cause the microwave to arc.*

Cutting

From orange dot:
- Cut 1 (2¼" by fabric width) binding strip for small cozy.

From blue dot:
- Cut 1 (2¼" by fabric width) binding strip for medium cozy.

From pink dot:
- Cut 2 (2¼" by fabric width) binding strips for large cozy.

From butterfly print:
- Cut 1 (14" by fabric width) strip.
    Subcut strip into 1 each 14" square, 10" square and 8" square.

From black-and-white dot:
- Cut 1 (14" by fabric width) strip.
    Subcut strip into 1 each 14" square, 10" square and 8" square.

From batting:
- Cut 2 each 14" squares, 10" squares and 8" squares.

Project Notes
Read all instructions before beginning this project.

Stitch right sides together using a ¼" seam allowance unless otherwise specified.

Materials and cutting lists assume 40" of usable fabric width for yardage.

Completing the Cozies

1. Pin each fabric square (butterfly print and black dot) to a same-size batting square with the fabric right side up as shown in Figure 1. Using matching thread, stitch diagonally from corner to corner to secure the layers.

Figure 1

2. Referring to Figure 2, fold one square in half with the fabric side in the center. Mark dart lines, referring to Dart Size Chart for specific measurements for each size square.

Square Size	Dart Size
8" x 8"	1" x 1¼"
10" x 10"	1" x 2¼"
14" x 14"	1" x 3¼"

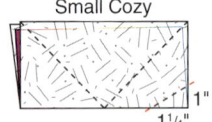

Figure 2

3. Stitch on the drawn dart lines, backstitching at both ends.

4. Fold the fabric the other direction and repeat Steps 2 and 3 to make a bowl-shaped unit with a dart on each side as shown in Figure 3.

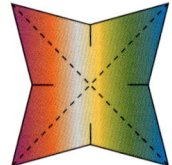

Figure 3

5. Repeat Steps 2–4 with the same-size batting-backed square to make two bowl-shaped units.

6. Referring to Figure 4, trim each dart to ¼" and then trim just the batting close to the dart seam.

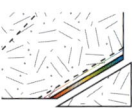

Figure 4

7. Nest two same-size bowl shapes (butterfly print and black dot) with wrong sides facing, matching the corners and dart seams. Fold the darts in opposite directions to nest and distribute the bulk and pin in place. Baste along the edge by hand or machine.

8. Fold and press the binding and apply to the raw edges by sewing the binding on the butterfly side. The two pink strips for the largest bowl will need joined before pressing. When approaching the dart area, pull the seam line straight to stitch the binding as shown in Figure 5. Fold the binding over to the black dot side. Hand-stitch the binding to the black dot side, mitering the corners and overlapping the ends to finish. ●

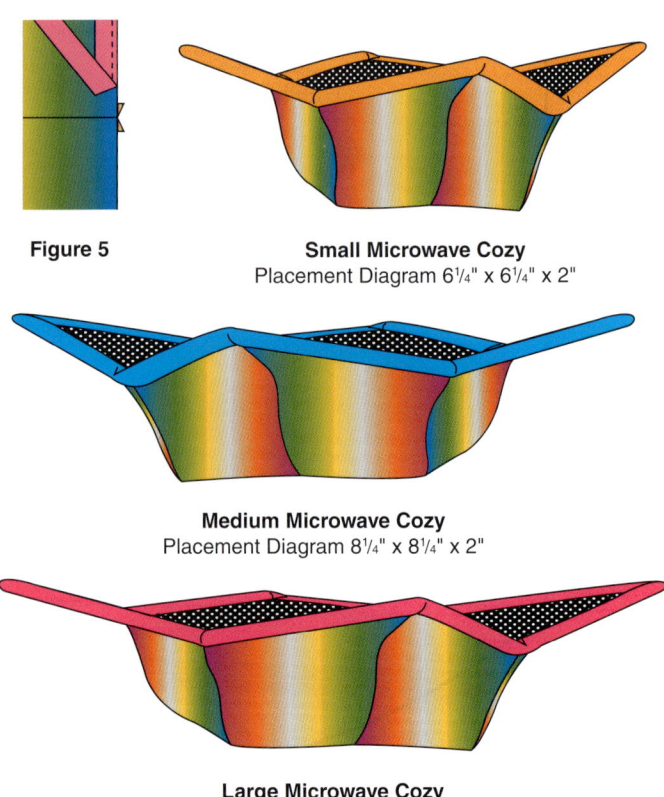

Figure 5

Small Microwave Cozy
Placement Diagram 6¼" x 6¼" x 2"

Medium Microwave Cozy
Placement Diagram 8¼" x 8¼" x 2"

Large Microwave Cozy
Placement Diagram 12¼" x 12¼" x 2"

Fresh Bread Bag

Design by Kathleen Berlew

This pretty and practical bread bag is a great way to practice piecing skills. Simple embroidery adds to its handmade appeal.

Skill Level:
Beginner

Finished Size
Bag Size: 8" x 16½"

Materials
- Fat eighth each aqua and pink prints
- ⅓ yard each yellow print and white solid
- Yellow, aqua and light plum embroidery floss
- 1¼ yards white ¼"-wide rickrack
- 1 (⅛"-diameter) cover button kit
- Tissue or tracing paper
- 2½" x 8½" rectangle iron-on fusible interfacing
- Thread

Project Notes
Read all instructions before beginning this project.

Stitch right sides together using a ¼" seam allowance unless otherwise specified.

Materials and cutting lists assume 40" of usable fabric width for yardage and 20" for fat eighths.

Cutting

From aqua print:
- Cut 2 (2½" x 8½") D rectangles.

From pink print:
- Cut 2 (2½" x 8½") E rectangles.

From yellow print:
- Cut 1 (8½" by fabric width) strip.
  Subcut strip into 1 (8½" x 17") backing rectangle, 1 (2½" x 8½") B rectangle, 1 (5" x 8½") C rectangle and 1 (3") G square.

From white solid:
- Cut 1 (8½" by fabric width) strip.
  Subcut strip into 2 (8½" x 17") F and 1 (2½" x 8½") A rectangle.

From white rickrack:
- Cut 6 (9") and 1 (4½") pieces.

Completing the Bag

1. Following manufacturer's instructions, fuse the iron-on interfacing to the wrong side of A.

2. Transfer the embroidery template onto the right side of A. With two strands of embroidery floss and using a backstitch, embroider lettering onto fabric as indicated on template.

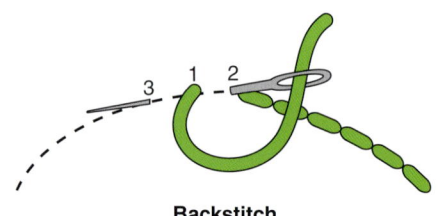

Backstitch

3. Arrange and sew A, B, C, D and E rectangles together to complete the bag front; press seams toward darker fabrics.

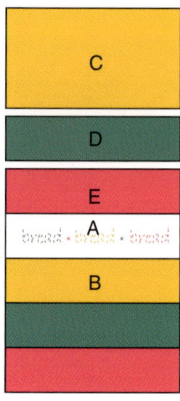

Figure 1

4. Sew a 9" piece of rickrack over each seam with matching thread. Trim rickrack edges even with fabric edges.

5. Referring to Figure 2, with right sides facing, sew bag front and backing rectangle together, along both sides and bottom edge. Trim seams and clip corners. Turn to right side.

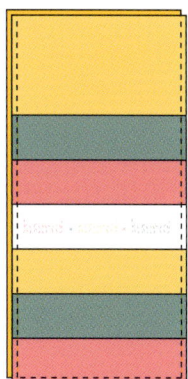

Figure 2

6. Repeat Step 5, sewing F rectangles together. Do not turn. Trim seams and clip corners.

7. Place outer bag inside lining with right sides facing. Fold 4½" piece of rickrack in half. Place folded loop between fabric layers, centered, at back of bag so raw edges of rickrack align with raw fabric edges. Pin in place.

8. Sew top edges of outer bag and lining together with ¼" seam, leaving an opening in front for turning. Trim seams and clip corners. Turn bag to right side and tuck lining inside outer bag. Whipstitch opening closed.

9. Following manufacturer's directions, use G square to make cover button.

10. Sew button to center of top D strip on front of bag. Fold over top panel of bag to fasten rickrack loop over button.

Note: *To make loop slightly tighter, tack sides of loop together close to fold.*

Fresh Bread Bag
Placement Diagram 8" x 16½"

Fresh Bread Bag
Bread Embroidery Template

Floral Fabric Baskets

Designed & Quilted by Chris Malone

These three baskets are so useful and decorative at the same time. They are easy to make and can be styled to fit any room.

Skill Level:
Confident Beginner

Finished Sizes
Large Basket Size: 15½" x 12½" x 6"

Medium Basket Size: 11½" x 10" x 5"

Small Basket Size: 9½" x 7½" x 4"

Materials
Materials listed make one set of three baskets (large, medium and small).

- Scraps each green, orange, red and blue tonals
- ⅓ yard blue dot
- ⅜ yard yellow dot
- ⅝ yard red dot
- 1½ yards ivory tonal
- 1½ yards batting
- 1 each (1½") red and orange buttons
- Black No. 8 pearl cotton thread or embroidery floss
- Template material
- Thread
- Basic sewing tools and supplies

Project Notes
Read all instructions before beginning this project.

Stitch right sides together using a ¼" seam allowance unless otherwise specified.

Materials and cutting lists assume 40" of usable fabric width for yardage.

Cutting

From each blue and orange tonal:
- Cut 1 (4" x 4½") C rectangle.

From blue dot:
- Cut 1 (10" by fabric width) strip.
  Subcut strip into 2 (10" x 14") small basket lining rectangles, 2 (2½" x 9") small basket handle strips and 1 (4½" x 5½") B rectangle.

From yellow dot:
- Cut 1 (17" by fabric width) strip.
  Subcut strip into 2 (12" x 17") medium basket lining rectangles, 2 (2½" x 9") medium basket handle strips and 1 (4½" x 5½") B rectangle.

From red dot:
- Cut 1 (22" by fabric width) strip.
  Subcut strip into 2 (16" x 22") large basket lining rectangles and 2 (2½" x 9") large basket handle strips.

From ivory tonal:
- Cut 1 (22" by fabric width) strip.
  Subcut strip into 2 (16" x 22") large basket A rectangles and 2 (2½" x 9") basket handles.
- Cut 1 (12" by fabric width) strip.
  Subcut strip into 2 (12" x 17") medium basket rectangles and 2 (2½" x 9") basket handles.
- Cut 1 (10" by fabric width) strip.
  Subcut strip into 2 (10" x 14") small basket rectangles and 2 (2½" x 9") basket handles.

From batting:
- Cut 2 (16" x 22") large basket rectangles.
- Cut 2 (12" x 17") medium basket rectangles.
- Cut 2 (10" x 14") small basket rectangles.
- Cut 6 (2½" x 9") basket handle strips.

Completing the Baskets

Large Basket With Flower & Butterfly
1. Baste a same-size batting rectangle to the wrong side of the two A rectangles by hand or machine, about ³⁄₁₆" from the edge. Quilt a 1" vertical grid on both pieces, or quilt as desired.

2. Cut a 3" square from the bottom corners of each rectangle as shown in Figure 1.

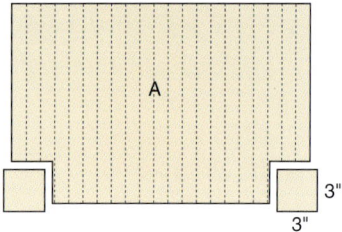

Figure 1

3. Prepare templates for the flower petal and leaf, using patterns provided.

4. Trace the petal pattern six times onto the wrong side of the red tonal. Referring to Figure 2, fold the fabric in half with the right sides facing and the pattern on top and pin to a batting scrap. Sew all around on pattern lines, leaving open at the bottom straight edge. Cut out ⅛" from the seam; trim the batting close to the seam and clip the curves. Turn right side out and press edges flat.

Figure 2

5. Arrange the petals in a tight circle about 2¾" from the top edge and 5" from the left edge of one of the quilted A rectangles as shown in Figure 3.

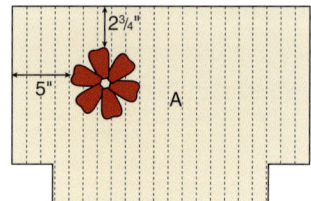

Figure 3

6. Referring to Figure 4, attach the flower by stitching three lines up each petal using red thread. Sew the red button to the flower center.

Figure 4

7. Trace the leaf pattern two times onto the wrong side of the green tonal. Fold the fabric in half with the right sides facing and the pattern on top and pin to a batting scrap. Sew all around on pattern lines. Cut out ⅛" from the seam, trim the batting close to the seam and clip the curves. Cut a slash where indicated on pattern through the top layer of fabric only as shown in Figure 5. Turn the leaf right side out and press the edges flat. Whipstitch the cut edges of the opening closed.

 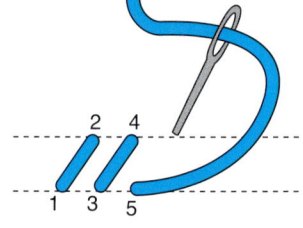

Figure 5

Whipstitch

8. Place the leaves between flower petals as shown in the photo and Placement Diagram. Attach the leaves by stitching vein lines using green thread.

9. To make the butterfly, refer to Figure 6 and fold the B rectangle in half, right sides facing, so it measures 4½" x 2¾" and sew the raw edges together, leaving a 2" opening on the long edge. Trim corners and turn right side out through the opening. Fold in the seam allowance on the opening and hand-stitch the folded edges together to close.

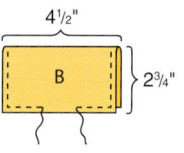

Figure 6

10. Thread a needle with a doubled strand of matching thread and sew a running stitch up the center of the rectangle as shown in Figure 7. Pull the thread to gather tightly and wrap the thread around the center twice before knotting in the back. Do not clip the thread.

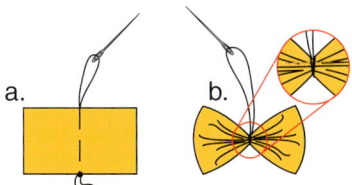

Figure 7

11. Repeat Steps 9 and 10 using the orange tonal B rectangle, folding it to a 4" x 2¼" rectangle and clipping the thread after knotting.

12. To assemble the butterfly, referring to Figure 8, place the larger yellow set of wings above the orange wings, overlapping slightly. Use the still attached thread to wrap around the center of the two wings until they are held together securely.

Figure 8

13. Place the butterfly to the right side of the flower as shown; mark the top center of the butterfly with a pin and remove the butterfly. Transfer the antennae pattern to the bag front and machine-stitch over the lines twice with black thread or stitch by hand with pearl cotton or embroidery floss.

14. To attach the butterfly, place the wings at the base of the antennae and use black pearl cotton or embroidery floss to make several stitches over the center of the wings, covering the thread.

15. If desired, use the same thread to quilt a loopy line from the butterfly to the flower with a large running stitch.

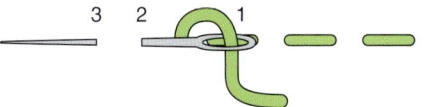

Running Stitch

16. Pin the bag front and back together, right sides facing, and stitch the side and bottom seams as shown in Figure 9; press seams open.

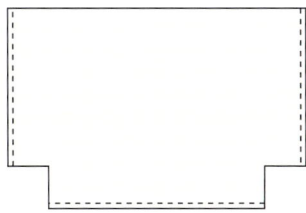

Figure 9

17. Referring to Figure 10, fold the bottom seam to the adjacent side seam, matching seam lines, and stitch a ¼" seam. Repeat on the other corner to make the boxed bottom. Turn basket right side out.

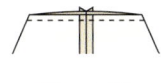

Figure 10

18. To make the handles, place the red dot strips right sides facing to ivory strips and pin each to a batting strip as shown in Figure 11. Sew on the two long edges. Trim the batting close to the seam and turn right side out. Press the edges flat and topstitch ¼" from the long edges.

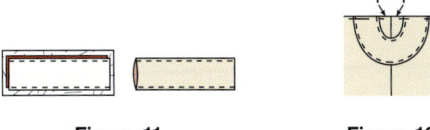

Figure 11   **Figure 12**

19. Referring to Figure 12, pin the ends of each handle 1" from the side seams of the basket with the red side down. Stitch across to hold.

20. To make the lining, cut a 3" square from the bottom corners of the two lining rectangles. Sew the side and bottom seams as in Step 16 but leave a 5" opening on the bottom seam. Box the bottom corners as in Step 17. Do not turn right side out.

21. Slip the basket inside the lining, right sides together, matching the side seams, and pin and sew all around at the top. Turn basket right side out through the opening in the bottom of the lining. Fold in the seam allowance on the lining opening and slip-stitch the folded edges together to close. Push the lining inside the basket and press the top edges flat.

22. Topstitch around the top of the basket ¼" from the edge to finish.

Medium Floral Fabric Basket
Placement Diagram 11½" x 10" x 5"

Small Basket With Butterfly

1. Follow Steps 1 and 2 for the Large Basket but make the cutouts 2" x 2".

2. Follow Steps 9–14 for the Large Basket butterfly using the blue dot and blue tonal fabrics and positioning the butterfly at an angle with the top corner about 1½" down from the top edge and 5½" from the left edge.

3. If desired, use the black thread to quilt a loopy line from the butterfly to the left side edge of the basket front with a large running stitch.

4. Follow Steps 16–22 using the blue dot lining pieces to complete the basket. ●

Large Floral Fabric Basket
Placement Diagram 15½" x 12½" x 6"

Medium Basket With Flower

1. Follow Steps 1 and 2 for the Large Basket but make the cutouts 2½" x 2½".

2. Follow Steps 3–8 for the Large Basket flower, using the orange tonal fabric and orange button and positioning the flower about 2" down and 4½" in from the left edge.

3. Follow Steps 16–22 for the Large Basket using the yellow dot lining pieces to complete the basket.

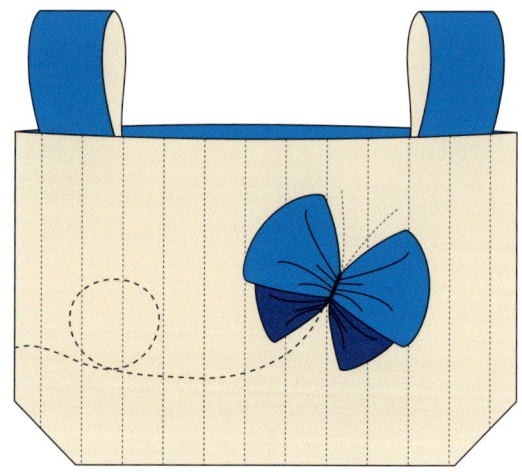

Small Floral Fabric Basket
Placement Diagram 9½" x 7½" x 4"

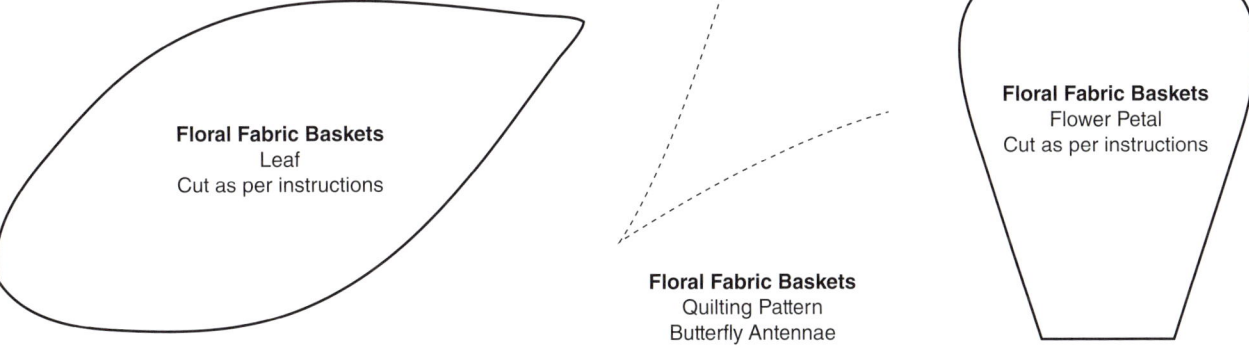

Floral Fabric Baskets
Leaf
Cut as per instructions

Floral Fabric Baskets
Quilting Pattern
Butterfly Antennae

Floral Fabric Baskets
Flower Petal
Cut as per instructions

AnniesCraftStore.com

Flower Eyeglasses Case

Design by Chris Malone

Sew a simple padded case for your glasses,
or store your rotary cutter safely inside!

Skill Level:
Beginner

Finished Size
Case Size: 4½" x 6¾"

Materials
- Scraps green tonal, light and dark pink dot
- 1 (4½" x 14") gray dot A rectangle
- 1 (4½" x 14") pink print B rectangle
- 2 (2¼" x 7½") gray tonal C strips
- 1 (4½" x 14") batting rectangle
- 3¼" length white elastic cord
- 1 (⅝") gray shank button
- Template material
- Fusible web with paper release
- Thread
- Basic sewing tools and supplies

Project Notes
Read all instructions before beginning this project.

Stitch right sides together using a ¼" seam allowance unless otherwise specified.

Completing the Case
1. Baste the batting rectangle to the wrong side of A.

2. Prepare templates for the flower, flower center, stem and leaf appliqués using the patterns provided.

3. Referring to Raw-Edge Fusible Appliqué on page 64, draw each of the appliqué shapes on the paper side of the fusible web. Apply the fusible web to the wrong side of the appliqué fabrics as listed below. Cut out the shapes on the pattern lines and remove the paper backing.

- Light pink dot: flower
- Dark pink dot: flower center
- Green tonal: stem and leaf

4. Arrange the appliqué on the right side of A with the flower about 1" down from the top edge and the top of the stem tucked ¼" under the flower. Fuse in place. Machine blanket-stitch around the appliqués using matching thread. Stitch a curved vein line in the leaf.

5. Fold the elastic cord in half and place the ends at the center bottom of the case with the ends even with the raw edges as shown in Figure 1. Stitch in place with shortened stitches to secure.

Figure 1

6. Referring to Figure 2, place the B rectangle over the appliquéd case, right sides facing, and stitch both short ends.

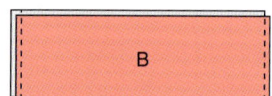

Figure 2

7. Trim the batting close to the seams and turn right side out; press the edges flat. Referring to Figure 3, topstitch ¼" from the seam on both ends and stitch across the case at the center point.

Figure 3

8. Fold the case in half with the lining sides facing and baste the sides together as shown in Figure 4.

Figure 4

9. Fold each C strip in half lengthwise, wrong sides facing, and press to prepare the binding for the sides.

10. Referring to Figure 5, stitch a binding strip to one side with the raw edges even with the case edges on the front and an equal overhang at the top and bottom. Repeat on the other side.

Figure 5 **Figure 6**

11. On the back side of the case, fold the overhang at the top and bottom in so it is even with the case and then fold the binding to the back side as shown in Figure 6. Hand-stitch the binding down to the back and slip-stitch the folded edges together at the top and bottom. Repeat on the other side.

12. Sew the button to the top center of the front of the case to finish. ●

Flower Eyeglasses Case
Placement Diagram 4½" x 6¾"

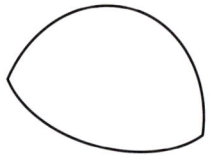

Flower Eyeglasses Case
Flower Center
Cut as per instructions

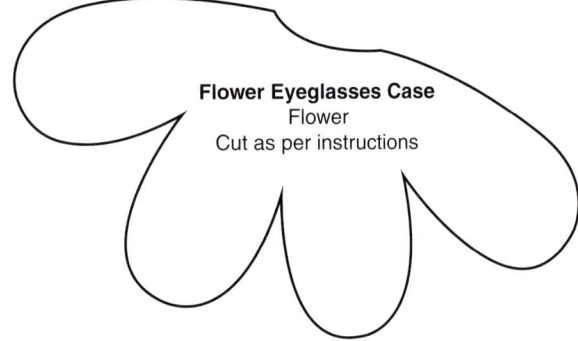

Flower Eyeglasses Case
Flower
Cut as per instructions

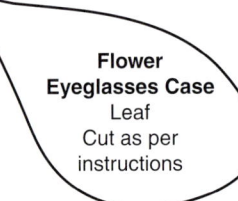

Flower Eyeglasses Case
Leaf
Cut as per instructions

Flower Eyeglasses Case
Stem
Cut as per instructions

Change Purse

Design by Sue Pfau of Sweet Jane's Quilting

This cute coin purse has no bottom corners or finished seams, making it a great project for a beginner. It makes the construction much faster and less complicated.

Skill Level:
Beginner

Finished Size
Purse Size: 5" x 3½"

Materials
Materials listed make one purse.
- Fat eighth floral print*
- Fat eighth orange tonal*
- 1 (6" x 9") fusible fleece rectangle
- 1 (7") nylon #3 coil zipper
- Template material
- Thread
- Basic sewing tools and supplies

*Gypsy fabrics by Jessica VanDenburgh for Windham used to make sample.

Project Notes
Read all instructions before beginning this project.

Stitch right sides together using a ¼" seam allowance unless otherwise specified.

Materials and cutting lists assume 20" of usable fabric width for fat eighths.

Cutting
Prepare template using provided pattern.

From floral print:
- Cut 1 A cutting template shape.

From orange tonal:
- Cut 1 B cutting template shape.

From fusible fleece:
- Cut 1 cutting template shape.

Completing the Purse

1. Following manufacturer's directions, fuse fleece to the wrong side of A.

2. Clip the zipper on each side a scant ¼" from the edge at 1" intervals.

3. With right sides together, pin the zipper across one curved end of A with both ends extending past the fabric as shown in Figure 1. Sew the zipper in place using a zipper foot.

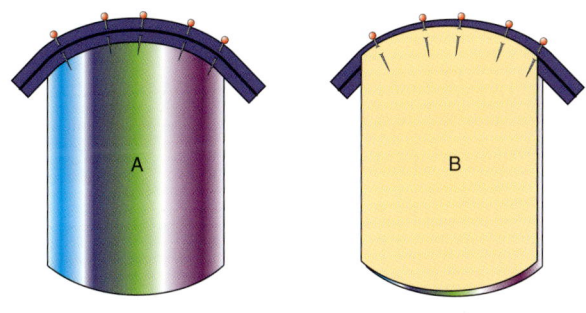

Figure 1   Figure 2

4. Referring to Figure 2, pin B over the zipper and into A, aligning raw edges of A and B. Sew B over the zipper and A.

5. Turn the fabric so right sides are facing out. Topstitch the fabric just below the zipper as shown in Figure 3.

Figure 3

6. Referring to Figure 4, fold the A fabric and pin the curved edge with the upper edge of the zipper. Stitch in place.

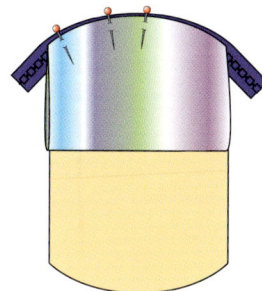

Figure 4

7. Repeat Step 6 with the B fabric as shown in Figure 5.

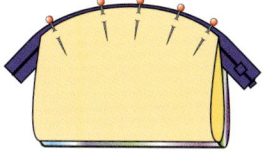

Figure 5

8. Unzip the pouch and turn it right side out. Topstitch the fabric just below the zipper.

9. Fold the pouch in half with the A fabric sides together. Zip the zipper closed 1½". Referring to Figure 6, align the sides and stitch the side edges closed.

Note: Sew from the bottom to the top, past the zipper teeth. Backstitch at the top, stitching over the zipper teeth to reinforce.

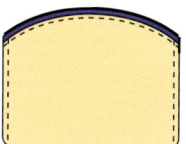

Figure 6

10. Clip zipper ends even with the pouch. Zigzag-stitch side seam allowances to finish seams.

11. Turn the purse right side out and poke out corners to finish. ●

Change Purse
Placement Diagram 5" x 3½"

Change Purse
Cutting Template
Cut as per instructions

Quilting Basics

The following is a reference guide. For more information, consult a comprehensive quilting book.

Quilt Backing & Batting

We suggest that you cut your backing and batting 8" larger than the finished quilt-top size. If preparing the backing from standard-width fabrics, remove the selvages and sew two or three lengths together; press seams open. If using 108"-wide fabric, trim to size on the straight grain of the fabric.

Prepare batting the same size as your backing. You can purchase prepackaged sizes or battings by the yard and trim to size.

Quilting

1. Press quilt top on both sides and trim all loose threads.
2. Make a quilt sandwich by layering the backing right side down, batting and quilt top centered right side up on flat surface and smooth out. Pin or baste layers together to hold.
3. Mark quilting design on quilt top and quilt as desired by hand or machine. **Note:** *If you are sending your quilt to a professional quilter, contact them for specifics about preparing your quilt for quilting.*
4. When quilting is complete, remove pins or basting. Trim batting and backing edges even with raw edges of quilt top.

Binding the Quilt

1. Join binding strips on short ends with diagonal seams to make one long strip; trim seams to ¼" and press seams open (Figure A).

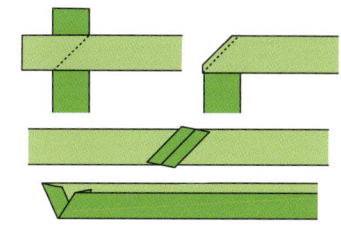

Figure A

2. Fold 1" of one short end to wrong side and press. Fold the binding strip in half with wrong sides together along length, again referring to Figure A; press.
3. Starting about 3" from the folded short end, sew binding to quilt top edges, matching raw edges and using a ¼" seam. Stop stitching ¼" from corner and backstitch (Figure B).

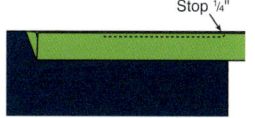

Figure B

4. Fold binding up at a 45-degree angle to seam and then down even with quilt edges, forming a pleat at corner, referring to Figure C.

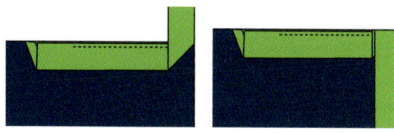

Figure C

5. Resume stitching from corner edge as shown in Figure C, down quilt side, backstitching ¼" from next corner. Repeat, mitering all corners, stitching to within 3" of starting point.
6. Trim binding end long enough to tuck inside starting end and complete stitching (Figure D).

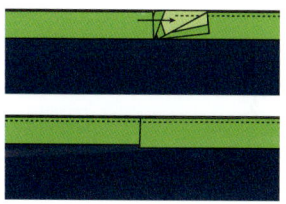

Figure D

7. Fold binding to quilt back and stitch in place by hand or machine to complete your quilt.

Raw-Edge Fusible Appliqué

One of the easiest ways to appliqué is the raw-edge fusible-web method. Paper-backed fusible web motifs or individual pieces are fused to the wrong side of fabric, cut out and then fused to a foundation fabric and stitched in place by hand or machine.

CUTTING APPLIQUÉ PIECES

1. Fusible appliqué motif pieces and individual pieces should be reversed for this technique.
2. Trace the appliqué shapes onto the paper side of paper-backed fusible web. Leave at least ¼" between shapes. Cut out shapes leaving a margin around traced lines. *Note: If doing several identical appliqués, trace reversed shapes onto template material to make reusable templates.*
3. Follow manufacturer's instructions and fuse shapes to wrong side of fabric as indicated on pattern for color and number to cut.
4. Cut out appliqué shapes on traced lines. Remove paper backing from shapes.
5. Again following fusible web manufacturer's instructions, arrange and fuse pieces to quilt referring to quilt pattern.

STITCHING APPLIQUÉ EDGES

Machine-stitch appliqué edges to secure the appliqués in place and help finish the raw edges with matching or invisible thread. Invisible thread can be used to stitch appliqués down when using the blanket or straight stitches. Do not use it for the satin stitch.

A short, narrow buttonhole or blanket stitch is most commonly used. Your machine manual may also refer to this as an appliqué stitch. Be sure to stitch next to the appliqué edge with the stitch catching the appliqué.

Practice turning inside and outside corners on scrap before stitching appliqué pieces. Learn how your machine stitches so that you can make the pivot points smooth.
1. To stitch outer corners, stitch to the edge of the corner and stop with needle in the fabric at the corner point. Pivot to the next side of the corner and continue to sew. You will often get a box on an outside corner.
2. To stitch inner corners, pivot at the inner point with needle in fabric. You will frequently see a Y shape in the corner.
3. You can also use a machine satin stitch or straight/running stitch. Turn corners in the same manner, stitching to the corners and pivoting with needle in down position.
4. Use a light- to medium-weight stabilizer behind an appliqué to keep the fabric from puckering during machine stitching.
5. To reduce the stiffness of a finished appliqué, cut out the center of the fusible web shape, leaving a ¼"-½" inside the pattern line. This gives a border of adhesive to fuse to the background and leaves the center soft and easy to quilt.
6. If an appliqué fabric is so light colored or thin that the background fabric shows through, fuse a lightweight interfacing to the wrong side of the fabric or fuse a piece of the appliqué fabric to a matching piece, wrong sides together, and then apply the fusible with a drawn pattern to one side.

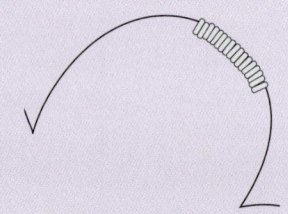

Satin Stitch

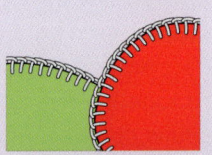

Blanket Stitch

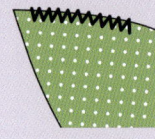

Zigzag Stitch

Published by Annie's, 306 East Parr Road, Berne, IN 46711. Printed in USA. Copyright © 2019, 2024 Annie's. All rights reserved. This publication may not be reproduced in part or in whole without written permission from the publisher.

RETAIL STORES: If you would like to carry this publication or any other Annie's publication, visit AnniesWSL.com.

Every effort has been made to ensure that the instructions in this publication are complete and accurate. We cannot, however, take responsibility for human error, typographical mistakes or variations in individual work. Please visit AnniesCustomerService.com to check for pattern updates.

ISBN: 978-1-64025-098-7
9 10 11 12 13 14